ART IN THE REAL WORLD

WHAT IS ARCHITECTURE?

JENNIFER LOMBARDO

ROSEN
PUBLISHING

Published in 2026 by The Rosen Publishing Group, Inc.
2544 Clinton Street, Buffalo, NY 14224

Portions of this work were originally authored by Don Nardo and published as *Architecture*. All new material this edition authored by Jennifer Lombardo.

Designer: Rachel Rising
Editor: Jennifer Lombardo

Cataloging-in-Publication Data

Names: Lombardo, Jennifer.
Title: What is architecture? / Jennifer Lombardo.
Description: Buffalo, NY : Rosen Publishing, 2026. | Series: Art in the real world | Includes glossary and index.
Identifiers: ISBN 9781499479331 (pbk.) | ISBN 9781499479348 (library bound) | ISBN 9781499479355 (ebook)
Subjects: LCSH: Architecture--Juvenile literature.
Classification: LCC NA200.L66 2026 | DDC 720.9--dc23

Manufactured in the United States of America

CPSIA Compliance Information: Batch #CWRYA26. For further information, contact Rosen Publishing at 1-800-237-9932.

CONTENTS

FOREWORD

Art is a uniquely human endeavor. After all, no other kind of animal creates art, at least not without human intervention, and no other animal seems to appreciate art as a human would. Art is such an essential part of the human experience that art forms are numerous: paintings, drawings, sculptures, jewelry, dance, and much more. As civilizations developed, art forms became more plentiful and some more complex, such as architecture, films, and theater. In fact, art surrounds us to such a degree now and in such a variety of ways that sometimes we do not notice art for what it is.

To recognize the art that exists beyond museum walls, people may need to ask themselves what art is. It is certainly a difficult term to define. Most might say they know art when they see it. But do they? They might only recognize the most conventional forms of it.

Every brand of dictionary will include a slightly different interpretation of art's definition, but most would say art is an often-visual expression of thoughts, feelings, or emotions that is created through imagination and skill. Using this definition, we can understand that a more complete list of art forms should include graffiti, anime, fashion design, graphic design, and much more. Debates around these topics have been passionate and thought-provoking, with some people strongly arguing that they are indeed art and others just as strongly arguing that they are not.

This series asks readers to open their eyes and their minds to less conventional forms of art. As readers are introduced to the history of each art form, how it evolved, and what it looks like today, they will develop an appreciation for the ability and creativity needed to master each. They will learn how an artist may hone their talent for each art, whether they need to pursue a formal education, tips to get started in the field, the practical business side of it, and about some of the people who have "made it" as a successful artist in the art form.

Included in each text are quotes from experts, complete with citations to provide readers with sources for further research. Full-color photographs illustrate key points, helping readers visualize important concepts. Recommended books and websites also encourage young artists to explore related topics in more depth so that they can gain a greater appreciation for the art all around them in the real world.

Architecture shapes the buildings around us, from the grand tomb of the Taj Mahal (shown here) to the house you live in.

INTRODUCTION

A BRIEF HISTORY

Humans have been building structures for millions of years, from basic huts to grand cathedrals. Over time, historians and archaeologists have been able to study these buildings to learn about past ways of life. Looking at architecture from a specific time period gives people today an idea of what everyday life was like for past societies in terms of available resources, technological advancement, and personal and religious necessities, as well as how knowledgeable and forward-thinking that particular community was. The different types of architecture throughout history have not only helped researchers gather information about specific past civilizations, but they have also helped shape architecture in today's world as well.

Architecture—the practice of designing, creating, and building a structure—serves several purposes within a community. Functionality, or usefulness, is the most important. These structures are built to provide a space for people to live, work, or be entertained in, and they must have whatever people need to fulfill that function. For example, a building cannot be used as a restaurant if it has no kitchen.

In addition to functionality, it is also important to consider the actual look and feel of the building. Architects often attempt to blend functionality with aesthetics, creating a building that is both useful and pleasing to look at. Even simple structures from past civilizations fascinate modern-day people because the story and reasoning behind each structural choice creates a form that has, in some way, influenced the decisions that are made in architecture today.

BEAUTIFUL BUILDINGS

A large part of creating a successful architectural structure is understanding and applying the science necessary to complete the form. While the methods of building a structure and the materials used have changed over time, the science behind creating a functional building has changed very little. For example, the ancient Egyptians used basic elements of geometry in creating the huge Pyramids of Giza (near modern Cairo). They also incorporated their knowledge from past experiences that helped them understand technical aspects of building, such as the tensile strength of wood, stone, and other natural materials. Later, the Greeks and Romans also employed learned technologies to

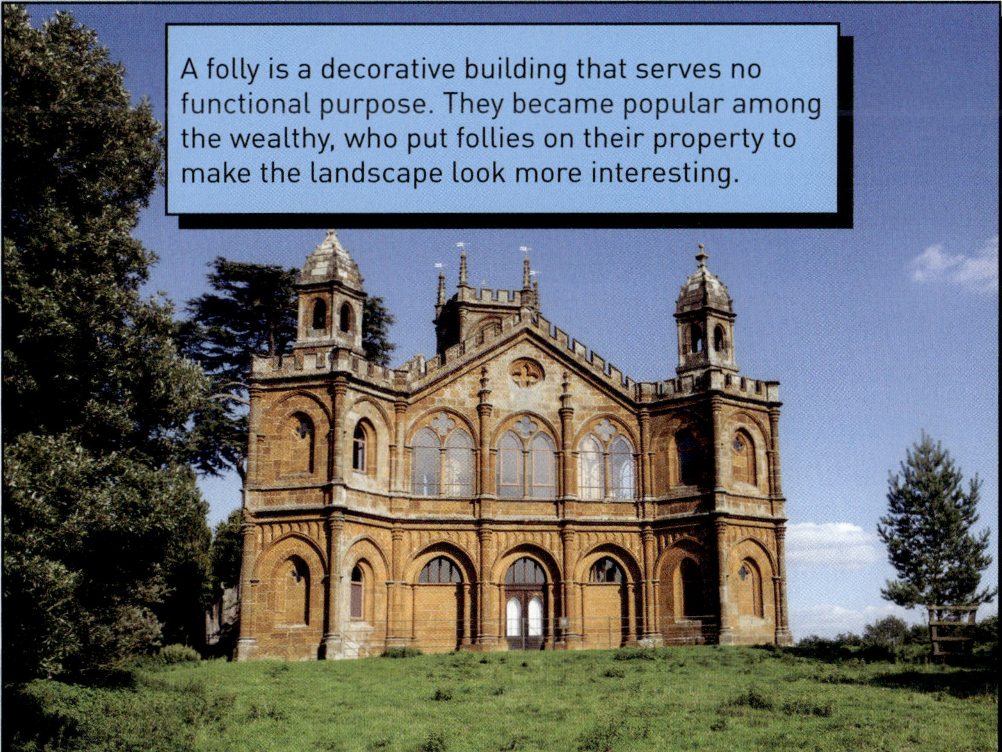

A folly is a decorative building that serves no functional purpose. They became popular among the wealthy, who put follies on their property to make the landscape look more interesting.

create monumental architecture. Each culture relied heavily on basic science to fuse their ideas into physical structures. In translated writing from the first century BCE, the Roman architect Vitruvius stated,

> *The science of the architect depends upon many disciplines … His personal service consists in craftsmanship and technology. Craftsmanship is a continued and familiar practice, which is carried out by the hands in such material as is necessary for the purpose of a design. Technology sets forth and explains things [made] in accordance with technical skill and method.*[1]

However, Vitruvius, who was educated in the impressive building techniques employed by Rome in his day, did not view a building merely as a technical, functional commodity. He also recognized the natural human desire for the structure to be aesthetically pleasing. The best architecture, he argued, should take full account of "grace, when the appearance of the work shall be pleasing and elegant, and the scale of the constituent parts is justly calculated by symmetry [visual balance]."[2]

Centuries later, the noted Italian Renaissance architect Leon Battista Alberti also stressed this basic need for artistic elements in architecture, saying,

> *There is a certain excellence and natural beauty in the figures and forms of buildings, which immediately strike the mind with pleasure and admiration. It is my opinion that beauty, majesty, gracefulness, and the like charms, consist in those particulars which if you alter or take away [those charms], the whole [would] be made homely [ugly] and disagreeable.*[3]

Thus, many great architects of the past believed that an effective piece of architecture must possess a balanced mixture of technological and artistic elements. This concept endured into the modern age. Many modern structures use materials more advanced than those available to past cultures, and a number of

Many people enjoy visiting beautiful buildings, such as the Royal Palace of Turin (shown here).

The Painted Ladies are a famous set of houses in San Francisco. Architects had to take the city's many hills into account.

modern buildings, particularly skyscrapers, look quite different than buildings from past ages. However, modern architects are just as aware as their predecessors were of the need to appeal to human aesthetic concerns. Today, as in the past, art and science "combine in all buildings," architectural critic James Neal pointed out. "Without science buildings are unlikely to have any structural permanence; if they lack art, people would not find them beautiful enough to allow them to remain over the years."[4]

INSIDE AND OUTSIDE

Neal correctly emphasized the human element, since both technology and art exist to serve people and their needs. Other types of art, such as painting and sculpture, do serve human needs by decorating rooms inside buildings for people's pleasure. Quite often, these arts are also used on the outside in architectural decoration. For example, the Ndebele women of Zimbabwe paint murals on the outside of their houses. The designs in the murals have meanings that represent the history of the Ndebele culture. However, architecture itself goes beyond the capabilities of other art forms because buildings are places for people to live and work in. Courtney Creenan-Chorley, AIA (American Institute of Architects), the president of the Buffalo Architecture Foundation in New York, noted some things architects must keep in mind when they design their buildings:

> *It is important to understand the needs of who will be using your building every day, how the weather and location interact with your building, and how your design interacts with other buildings, streets, parks, and spaces around it. Architecture is about making lives better by designing inspiring, functional, and comfortable spaces.*[5]

Because buildings are created for humans to live, work, and play inside, architecture must create enough space to accommodate them and their activities. It might be just enough space for a single family to use, or it might be the huge amount of space needed for people to hold public meetings, attend plays and concerts, or watch sporting events.

Either way, architecture itself is sometimes said to "live in," or be physically defined by, three-dimensional space. For this reason, the three-dimensional interior of a space is just as important as the exterior. These ideas are a large part of the architect's thought process when creating initial ideas for a structure.

BLENDING SCIENCE AND ART

Architecture is a tool that fulfills both the functional needs and artistic enjoyment of the people who use it to create their buildings. The communities in which those people live often make up a regional or national unit—or even an entire civilization, with its own unique political, economic, intellectual, and artistic aspirations. A great building or architectural style is an example of the achievements and power of that community, people, or civilization. In such cases, Neal wrote, architecture "is the ultimate mark of confidence in the power and culture of a society; from the Pyramids of Giza to the great palaces and cathedrals of Europe or to their modern equivalents, the museums and municipal buildings of our cities."[6]

The Parthenon temple, for instance, was more than a beautiful building paying homage to the goddess Athena. It was also a symbol of the power and glory of ancient Athens—a boast, as well as a warning, to other nations of that time and era. Similarly, today, giant skyscrapers symbolize the wealth, power, and achievements of both the people who create them and those communities in which they stand.

Architectural styles around the world are often shaped by the styles of the past, but they are also determined by the climate, geography, economy, and availability of materials in different parts of the world. For most of history, architects have had to figure out how to make buildings both beautiful and functional using limited materials. In northern Europe, especially Germany and France, a style of house called a half-timbered house was popular from about the 1100s to the 1900s. Wood was widely available in these areas and was less expensive than stone, so builders would make a house with a wooden frame and then fill in the frame with brick or plaster. The wood could be arranged in different patterns, and flowers or other designs were often carved into the plaster for decoration.

Architecture is a combination of scientific technology and artistic expression that a given community of individuals embraces, shapes, and adapts to its own needs and desires. At the same time, great buildings become leading symbols of those people and their accomplishments. Perhaps no one has summed it up better than the late Frank Lloyd Wright, one of the greatest architects of the 20th century. "The sciences cannot benefit human beings, really," he said, "until creative art takes them up and shows how to use them according to human quality and interests."[7] In other words, Wright stated that although science is the most important aspect of achieving and physically creating an architectural form, it is nothing without the personal connections and creative thoughts of not only the architect, but the community that surrounds him or her.

Fallingwater is one of Frank Lloyd Wright's most famous works.

CHAPTER ONE

EARLY ARCHITECTURE

Architecture was not always considered an art form. At first, it was simply a way to fill humans' need for shelter. Materials used for these structures were mainly found in the surrounding habitat, which did not leave much room for architectural innovation. Though they were small and simple, historians have learned a great deal about the history of architecture from these early beginnings.

This age of beginnings for civilization, moving toward the end of the "stone age," is known as the Neolithic period. It ranged from 10,000 to 2000 BCE. A new and different way of life began in this age. Farming replaced hunting and gathering, which had forced people to stay on the move. Shelters had been simple and easy to move before; now, they needed to be sturdy enough to stay up for years. Other buildings that a static, or unmoving, society needs or enjoys—including meeting halls, places to cook and eat, and religious temples—also began to appear. Basic architectural styles and structural sciences began to form, which eventually evolved into more complex ideas that are still used today.

Jericho, a city located in what is now Israel, was one of the first known towns of architectural significance. Its rounded houses, created from mud bricks, became the foundation from which innovative architecture emerged. During this same time period, an architectural form now referred to as the post and lintel was created. It consists of two vertical supports, the posts (also called pillars or piers), topped by a horizontal beam or slab, the lintel. At first, such units were composed of wood. However, they later came to be made of more durable and permanent stone, too. The post and lintel became a crucial component of most large-scale buildings that followed because it allowed people to construct doors and windows in structures and gateways in walls. Most temples, palaces, forts, battlements, and other buildings would have been impossible to create without this basic architectural concept.

FENDING OFF ATTACKERS

Both the beginnings of agriculture and the rise of the first towns and cities took place in a region that is now called the Middle East. In ancient times, the region encompassed what is now Turkey; what are now Syria, Palestine, and Israel, on the eastern coast of the Mediterranean Sea; Egypt, the northern coast of which also borders the Mediterranean; and lying east of these areas, the mostly flat plains of Mesopotamia—occupied today by Iraq and some surrounding areas.

Among the first Neolithic towns in these areas was an agricultural settlement in southeastern Anatolia, also referred to as Asia Minor, which was located in modern-day Turkey. Modern archaeologists have named it Çatalhöyük. It is believed to have been founded around 8000 BCE but to have reached its greatest size and level of prosperity in the seventh and sixth millennia BCE. Covering some 32 acres (13 ha), Çatalhöyük is certainly the largest known Neolithic site in the Middle East. A number of experts view it as the first clear example of communal architecture. The town consisted of a monolithic complex of brick houses connected to one another.

Marvin Trachtenberg and Isabelle Hyman described the overall look of the structures:

> *The houses were entered through a hole in the roof that was at once chimney and doorway. Movement from house to house took place only over and through the roof … Packed into a continuous cellular structure, the houses presented a solid blank wall to the outside. The defensive compactness and structural economy of this architectural program were successful. Excavations revealed … [no] signs that the unusual wealth of the [town] had been plundered.*[8]

Çatalhöyük is so old that it was buried over time. Shown here is the present-day archaeological site.

In the same period in which Çatalhöyük reached its peak, Jericho was flourishing as well. Unlike Çatalhöyük, its small houses of mud bricks were not connected. Jericho's means of defense against security threats was instead an even greater architectural achievement—a towering defensive wall constructed of stone blocks. Some parts of this wall are still standing, reaching a height of 12 feet (3.6 m). The structure may have originally stood 20 to 25 feet (6 to 7.5 m) high. There was also at least one stone guard tower 30 feet (9 m) high. Over time, similar monumental defensive walls were built all over the area.

FROM SETTLEMENTS TO CITIES

Çatalhöyük is considered one of the world's first cities. Experts believe its population could have topped 10,000 at its height, which was a huge number for that time period. Other early cities were built in Mesopotamia by people today referred to as the Sumerians. Among the leading Sumerian cities were Ur, Uruk, Lagash, and Nippur, all clustered near the shores of the Persian Gulf. By 3600 BCE, each of these cities covered several square miles and supported a population in the tens of thousands. These are often considered to be the world's first true civilizations. Çatalhöyük and Jericho are typically considered proto-cities, or early versions of a city. The difference between a city and a proto-city is that a proto-city lacks organization and centralized government. A city is carefully planned and governed; a proto-city is simply a group of people living together.

Like Jericho, the Sumerian cities had large-scale defensive walls and battlements for security purposes. However, unlike Jericho's stone walls, those surrounding Ur and its neighbors were made of clay bricks. This is because the region known then as Mesopotamia has very few deposits of natural stone. Some of the bricks featured a mixture of clay and straw or sand, which provided some added strength. People pressed the clay or clay mixture into molds, then placed the molds outside and allowed the sun to dry them. The city walls constructed of these bricks were nothing less than architectural wonders for their time. Most, such as those at Uruk, were at least 6 miles

Varanasi, India, is one of the oldest continuously inhabited cities in the world. Some buildings are ancient; others are newer.

(10 km) in circumference, and a few eventually reached nearly twice that size.

The cities of Mesopotamia—both under the Sumerians and later local peoples, including the Babylonians and Assyrians—featured other forms of monumental architecture besides defensive walls. For example, every city in the area had one or more structures devoted to religious worship. These communal structures were temples, each dedicated to one or more gods or goddesses.

Some temples were constructed beside or atop enormous pyramid-like structures called ziggurats. A ziggurat was a solid brick structure that had one or more large stairways or ramps that priests and kings walked up. These high-ranking officials performed religious rituals in a small chapel or temple at the top.

In addition to their religious functions, ziggurats had a political use. Because of their great size—for example, the one at Ur was some 210 feet (64 m) long, 150 feet (46 m) wide, and likely more than 100 feet (30 m) high—they were time-consuming and expensive to build. This made them symbols of wealth, power, and prestige for those cities that could afford to build them.

Palaces to house local kings and their families were another architectural form that the leaders of Mesopotamian cities built to display their wealth and power. A typical palace in the region consisted of several rooms grouped around

THE TOMB OF KING TUT

The Valley of the Kings was the final burial place for many kings in the New Kingdom, a period of time in Egyptian history from around 1500 to 1000 BCE. One king in particular was named King Tutankhamun, commonly referred to as King Tut. His tomb was found in 1922 by Howard Carter, who chiseled through a doorway that led to the inside of the burial chamber. A vast amount of artifacts and information were gathered from the chamber, giving archaeologists an insight into family relationships in ancient Egypt. In 2015, evidence from radar scans suggested that more rooms could be present on the other side of Tutankhamun's tomb. Some experts believed these rooms housed Nefertiti, an Egyptian queen whose resting place has never been found. Further scans were performed and failed to provide clear evidence that there were other rooms behind King Tut's walls. Although some experts hold out hope, many believe the matter has been laid to rest for good.

a central unroofed courtyard. The throne room, meeting halls, and various storage and work facilities were most often located on the ground floor, while one or more upper stories housed the royal bedchambers and other living spaces.

THE EVOLUTION OF PYRAMIDS

There is some debate among experts as to who created the first true civilization: the Sumerians or the Egyptians, whose cities were built around the same time and also contained impressive architectural works. The most famous of these structures are the giant pyramids created as tombs for Egyptian kings, who were called pharaohs. Egypt's pyramid-tombs evolved from an earlier, smaller kind of tomb called a mastaba. Rectangular in shape, mastabas were used to bury deceased nobles and, like many structures in Mesopotamia, were composed of clay bricks. Because these bricks disintegrated rapidly, they needed frequent repairs. It was also fairly easy for tomb robbers to use stone or metal tools to tunnel through the crumbling walls, which was a problem because each pharaoh was buried with a large selection of their personal riches and belongings. To make the tombs of the nobility more permanent and secure, Egyptian builders increased the size of these structures. They also began making them from stone, which was far more durable and more difficult to penetrate than clay bricks.

In an effort to further solve the problem, an alternative burial site was created for the kings. This site, known today as the Valley of the Kings, was home to a different kind of architecture that focused not on the exterior, but exclusively on the interior structure. The tombs housed in this valley were hidden among natural rock structures in the middle of the mountains west of the Nile River. The entrances were plain and natural to try to fool grave robbers into thinking the tombs were not there. The inside had long corridors with steep drop-offs leading to individual burial chambers. Each architectural choice in these tombs was meticulously thought out and made with the security of the mummies and their belongings in mind.

Around 2630 BCE, Imhotep, architect to the pharaoh Djoser, stacked six stone mastabas on top of one another, each slightly smaller than the one below. The result was the world's first pyramid, today called the Step Pyramid of Djoser. Several other step pyramids were built in the years that followed. Eventually, builders began filling in the notches of the steps, producing the first smooth-sided, or "true," pyramids.

The most imposing and famous of the pyramids built in Egypt are the three at Giza. The largest, the tomb of the pharaoh Khufu, originally stood 481 feet (147 m) high, more than 2.5 times taller than the Statue of Liberty. The structure measured 756 feet (230 m) on each side and covered more than 13 acres (5 ha) of ground. The other two Giza pyramids—of Khufu's son, Khafre, and Khafre's successor, Menkaure—soared to 471 feet (143 m) and 218 feet (66 m), respectively.

These tombs and Egypt's few other surviving pyramids are among the oldest examples of great architecture in the world.

The temples on Malta are among the oldest freestanding buildings.

While many other notable human structures have come and gone, the giants of Giza and the carefully executed tombs remain, and they are likely to survive for undetermined ages to come.

LARGE AND PRIMITIVE

During the third millennium BCE, when the peoples of Mesopotamia and Egypt were building pyramids, temples, tombs, and other imposing architectural wonders, Europe also produced some monumental structures. These have come to be called megalithic. The term comes from the Greek words *megas*, meaning "great," and *lithos*, meaning "stone," because they are composed of enormous irregular stones, many weighing 10, 20, or 50 tons (9, 18, or 45 mt).

Europe's megalithic monuments were built by small cultures that existed roughly between 4000 and 1500 BCE. The most notable examples were built on the Mediterranean islands of Malta, Sardinia, and Sicily, as well as in Spain, Portugal, France, England, Ireland, and Scotland. Large underground tombs made of immense stones have been found in all these places. Aboveground megalithic religious temples were also created. One of the most striking is Hagar Qim, on Malta, built in about 3000 BCE. It features six spacious circular rooms and several stone altars, which were dedicated to a mother goddess associated with fertility.

More familiar among Europe's megalithic structures are cromlechs, which are large circles formed by evenly spaced upright stones. Most famous of all is Stonehenge in southern England, which was constructed in about 2500 BCE. Parts of the monument have fallen over the centuries, but much of it still remains. Originally, it consisted of a series of massive upright stone slabs topped by huge lintel stones that ran around the entire circumference. The purpose of Stonehenge is still debated. A widely accepted theory is that it was a sort of astronomical observatory; others suggest it was used for religious worship or as a symbol of political unity. Being such a historical mystery, Stonehenge is a popular spot for tourists to visit and is studied extensively by historians in hopes of providing more insight into the people who created it.

MINOAN ACHIEVEMENTS

Although the builders of Europe's megalithic structures were accomplished both technologically and artistically, they did not build a civilization in the classic sense. That is, they did not have cities, nations, forms of writing, and things made out of metal, as the Egyptians and Mesopotamians did. Europe's first true civilization in this sense belonged to the Minoans. These non-Greek-speaking people inhabited the large Greek island of Crete and other nearby islands in the Aegean Sea from about 2000 to 1500 BCE. This time period is referred to as Greece's Middle Bronze Age, when people used tools and weapons made of bronze—an alloy, or combination, of copper and tin. This new material created many new opportunities for expanding the technology and practice of architecture.

Among the many contributions the Minoans made to monumental architecture were several enormous, complex, palace-like structures that were used for public entertaining and celebrating. Each covered many acres and featured asymmetrical, multistoried, often split-level clusters of rooms, all arranged around a large central courtyard. These structures included several intricate staircases both in the interior and exterior of the building. Among other refinements, the Minoan palaces had advanced plumbing and drainage systems that both piped in clean water and removed wastes.

The purpose of these structures was not simply to provide luxurious accommodations for Minoan leaders. The palace-like structures were also the focus of community life and activities, including religious worship and sporting events. The central courtyard, archaeologist William R. Biers pointed out, "may have served as the site of processions, religious rituals, and other ceremonial functions and perhaps of the bull games [in which young men and women leaped over the backs of giant bulls] that we know from artistic representations."[9]

The Minoans exerted considerable cultural influence over the first Greek speakers in the region: the Mycenaeans, who

Knossos is a Minoan palace that is so well-preserved, some wall paintings were still visible when it was discovered. Many of these paintings were touched up by restorers.

UNIQUELY DESIGNED TOMBS

In addition to their monumental palace-citadels, the Mycenaeans built unique stone structures—tholos tombs—to bury their deceased royalty. Archaeologist William R. Biers of the University of Missouri provided this concise description:

> *Nowhere is Mycenaean construction seen to better advantage than in the great tholos or beehive tombs of the [Greek] mainland, which were in fact the royal burial vaults associated with the [Mycenaean] palace sites ... Tholos tombs were constructed of great blocks of cut stone and have been described as stone-lined holes. A deep circular cut in a hillside was lined with blocks laid in a corbel style [having each successive block slightly overhang the one below], so that the diameter of the circle decreased until the final opening at the top could be closed with a capstone.*[1]

1. William R. Biers, *The Archaeology of Greece*. Ithaca, NY: Cornell University Press, 1996, pp. 74, 76.

dwelled on the Greek mainland. The Mycenaeans built imposing palace-citadels made of giant irregular stones similar to those used by Europe's megalithic builders. These structures, along with the Cretan structures, were abandoned when the Minoan-Mycenaean civilization fell about 1100 BCE. The region of Greece then entered a long cultural dark age. Several centuries passed before a new civilization arose there—one whose unique new architectural forms have had a profound influence on world architecture.

CHAPTER TWO

REGIONAL STYLES

Around the same time that the Egyptians were building their pyramids, cultures in what is now known as central and eastern Asia began making their mark on the architectural world. These cultures developed the skills necessary to create some of the most monumental structures in history. This area encompassed what is now India, China, Japan, Cambodia, Thailand, Vietnam, and other nearby regions. Though their architectural styles were different than those of Mesopotamia, they had similar ideals that mostly consisted of the need for a communal space for religious practices.

Western styles tended to change significantly over time, while Eastern ones, after attaining an initial level of development, remained more or less the same. "Instead of a series of styles and trends," Neal pointed out,

> *the architecture of Eastern civilizations remained static for many centuries, much as that of the ancient Egyptians … [Partly because of] their strong philosophical religions, there was no need for the usual Western diversity of styles. The East developed a style that fitted its divine requirements and they felt no need to diverge from this path.*[10]

Despite these differences, the civilizations of the East and West shared one basic and important architectural theme: The central focus of their monumental architecture was the religious temple or shrine. These architectural masterpieces were created with an immense amount of detail in hopes of pleasing the gods they worshipped. Since religion—particularly Hinduism and Buddhism—was so highly regarded in these areas of the world, cultures expanded as these religions spread, creating a wider network of architectural ideas. These ideas played off of each other, meaning that many elements were borrowed from different civilizations and adapted to each different culture. These adaptations were made to incorporate specific elements that were believed to be sacred to each individual belief system.

DEATH AND RELIGION

The Asian equivalent of ziggurats and pyramids was the stupa. The basic form of the stupa originated somewhere in southern Asia, perhaps in the first millennium BCE or earlier. At first, stupas were burial mounds; the largest of the mounds was used to bury royalty. However, over time, stupas became more architecturally sturdy and elaborate, often having an intricate underlying design that was believed to represent the heavens or gods they worshipped. Fired bricks or stone blocks were stacked around the mound and sometimes were plastered and painted. The stupas, created to honor Buddha, or "the enlightened one," looked like round domes. People would come to these structures for the purpose of religious worship, which consisted of walking around the stupa in a clockwise direction.

Following Buddha's death, Buddhism spread swiftly to neighboring lands, including China, Thailand, Cambodia, Korea, and eventually Japan. The new faith had a tremendous influence on the development of Asian architecture. Stupas, for example, were transformed into shrines that symbolically linked Buddha's remains and enlightened ideas to the cosmos. Buddhist stupas were constructed by the thousands across Southeast Asia and became a dominant trademark of the faith.

Among the more outstanding examples is the Great Stupa at Sanchi, in north-central India. It is an impressive 120 feet (37 m) across and 54 feet (16.5 m) high, and it was built in the third century BCE by the ruler Ashoka. University of Washington scholar Francis D.K. Ching described it as "a solid mass built up in the form of hundreds of stone rings [each composed of individual stone blocks] that were surfaced with plaster and painted."[11] The purpose of the structure was to house relics—religious artifacts—of Buddha. In the first century BCE, alterations were made to the structure, adding more detail as well as a balustrade, or a railing held up by a system of posts. The greatest detail was in the sculpted carvings that were created to honor Buddha. The gateway to the stupa, for example, was carved with very intricate scenes that included people, animals, and other things that played an important role in the religion. The Great

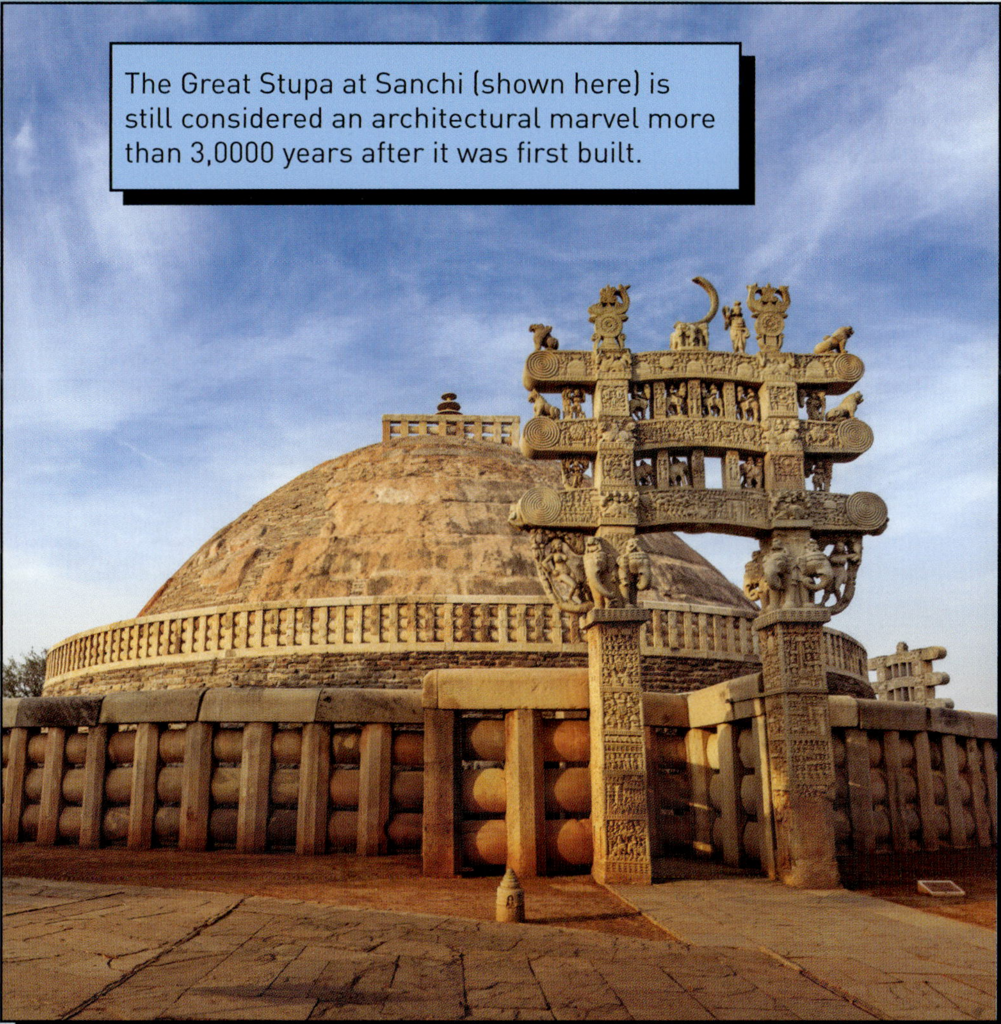

The Great Stupa at Sanchi (shown here) is still considered an architectural marvel more than 3,0000 years after it was first built.

Stupa at Sanchi exemplifies a key element to architecture in that this structure, though created many years ago, still holds value to the people of its culture.

CHANGES OVER TIME

Early Buddhist stupas such as the Great Stupa at Sanchi had a profound influence on most of the Far Eastern cultures that followed. These structures became architectural models that were copied, with some variations and refinements, again and again for years to come. The basic design elements of Buddhist stupas can be seen in Buddhist temples across Southeast Asia. The initial concept of the structure was kept, but refinements to the architectural elements created buildings that looked very different. One of the largest and most beautiful examples is the Shwezigon Pagoda, completed in Burma (now called Myanmar, located west of Thailand) in 1102 CE. A pagoda is a tower consisting of several separate tiers, or levels, stacked atop one another. In some areas it became customary to stack a stupa on top of a series of decorated tiers, producing a pagoda. Thus, the Shwezigon structure's stupa, covered in gold, sits atop three elaborately decorated, square-shaped tiers, each featuring an outer walkway. The entire temple is 160 feet (49 m) high and the same distance across at the base.

The stupa form also served as a basis for many of the Hindu temples in India. An early form of Hinduism, the Vedic faith, arose in India several centuries before Buddhism did. After Buddhism spread from India to other lands, Vedic worshippers steadily absorbed its ideals and eventually worshipped Buddha, making him an incarnation, or earthly form, of their great god Vishnu. This combination of Buddhism and the Vedic faith eventually became more like the form of Hinduism that is practiced today.

The Hindu gods are noticeable architectural elements in Hindu temples. Besides Vishnu and Buddha, other leading Hindu deities include Brahma, the creator; Shiva, the destroyer; and the elephant-headed Ganesh. Crowded groups of statues and carved reliefs of these and other Hindu gods became standard decorations on the outsides and insides of Hindu temples. Worshippers

The stupa is still a commonly used design. This one was built in 1991.

viewed them as divine guardians. Most Hindu temples also came to feature *shikharas*—pagoda-like towers that were essentially vertical extensions of the stupa form. In fact, Hindu shikharas became the model for the pagodas that steadily rose across China and Japan when Buddhism spread through these lands. The oldest surviving Buddhist pagoda in China is part of the Songyue Temple at Dengfeng in the northeastern part of the country, which was built in the sixth century. The pagoda has 12 sides, stands 131 feet (40 m) high, and has 15 stacked tiers.

ANGKOR WAT

Most of the Buddhist and Hindu temples and shrines built across Asia in the centuries following Buddha's death were nothing less than astonishing. However, none compare in size and glory to Angkor Wat, originally a Hindu temple complex at Angkor, Cambodia. It was built in the 12th century CE by Suryavarman II, a king of the powerful Khmer Empire, which encompassed a large portion of Southeast Asia from about CE 800 to 1430. The structure was originally a Hindu temple dedicated to Vishnu. Later it became a Buddhist temple. Today, Angkor Wat is a popular tourist attraction, but it is no longer used as a temple.

Among the first European visitors to Angkor Wat was a Portuguese friar who saw it in 1586. "[It] is of such extraordinary construction that it is not possible to describe it with a pen," he said, "particularly since it is like no other building in the world. It has towers and decoration and all the refinements which the human genius can conceive of."[12] A later French traveler was equally impressed, remarking that the temple rivaled the greatest architectural works of ancient Greece and Rome. This assessment is no exaggeration, considering Angkor Wat covers an immense area measuring 400 acres (161 ha) and features 5 huge shikharas, the tallest of which is 699 feet (213 m) high. In addition, the temple walls contain tens of thousands of square feet of sculptures showing the adventures of Hindu gods and heroes.

Angkor Wat is among a few structures that, because of their sheer size and scope, exemplified the ideals and practices for architecture in Asia. Another example is the Great Wall of China. An English lord who saw it in 1793 declared,

> *It is certainly the most stupendous work of human hands, for I imagine that if the outline of all the masonry of all the forts and fortified places in the whole world were to be calculated, it would fall considerably short of that of the Great Wall of China.*[13]

The Great Wall is not actually one single structure, but a collection of several different walls. Different Chinese rulers constructed these walls over a span of around 1,800 years, beginning in the third century BCE, mainly to discourage raids by enemy tribes living north and northwest of China. Their combined length is about 13,170 miles (21,195 km). Almost 30,000 guard towers and signal towers have survived. A watchman would light a fire to warn his people of enemy raiders, and watchmen in nearby towers passed the warning along by lighting their own fires. Large portions of the surviving walls are about 20 feet (6 m) thick and up to 28.5 feet (8.7 m) high. At first, most of the walls were made of pressed earth, clay, and sand mixed with water and highly compacted to form

Angkor Wat is just one of more than 1,000 temples in Angkor Archaeological Park.

building blocks. Later sections of the wall used stronger brick and stone construction. It is easy to see why these amazing monumental constructions were such effective defenses.

MESOAMERICAN PYRAMIDS

Although pyramids are strongly associated with Egypt and Mesopotamia, they were also built by cultures that existed in what are now Mexico, parts of the southern United States, and parts of Central America. The first advanced civilizations in this area, which is known as Mesoamerica, arose in the early first millennium BCE. It is believed that early worship there occurred on hilltops. Over time, it became customary to create large earthen mounds as substitutes for sacred hilltops. These mounds later developed into pyramids.

In some ways, the Mesoamerican pyramids resemble Mesopotamian ziggurats and Egypt's step pyramid. All three versions consist of several stepped levels, each smaller than the ones below it. However, the American pyramids are different than their counterparts in some key ways. First, each level of the step pyramid rises at nearly a right angle to the top of the level below it. In contrast, succeeding levels in Mesoamerican pyramids slope inward at a distinct angle, producing a more streamlined look. Also, the Mesoamerican pyramids were constructed differently than pyramids in other lands. The Pyramids of Giza were huge masses of piled stones; the ziggurat at Ur was a huge pile of sun-dried bricks. Most Mesoamerican pyramids, however, consisted of a network of stone walls contained within an outer stone wall, with dirt and rubble packed into the spaces between the walls.

One of the largest and the most architecturally influential of the Mesoamerican pyramids is the Pyramid of the Sun. It stood in the middle of a gigantic ceremonial center at Teotihuacán in Mexico's central highlands and is still in a remarkably fine state of preservation. The city of

The pyramids at Teotihuacán are a popular tourist attraction.

CONSPIRACY THEORIES

The scale of structures such as pyramids in Egypt and Mesoamerica has made some people wonder how and why they were built. People have suggested that the pyramids were built by aliens, that the existence of pyramids in different cultures proves ancient civilizations had close contact with each other, and many other wild theories. The rise of AI has helped conspiracy theorists create fake evidence to convince others that their ideas are true.

Scientists, historians, and archaeologists don't have all the answers about ancient civilizations, but they do know that all pyramids were built using math, science, and hard physical work. Conspiracy theorists tend to have difficulty understanding how advanced past civilizations were, leading them to incorrect assumptions. This is especially common when people discuss cultures outside of Europe, as racism often makes people believe that white cultures were far more advanced than non-white cultures.

Conspiracy theorists also tend to ignore facts that disprove their theories. For example, conspiracy theorists may say things such as "These civilizations had no way to build these structures," while ignoring the tools, quarries, and other evidence that archaeologists have found. They often try to deflect attention away from their lack of evidence by claiming that scientists don't want people to know "the truth" and that they are "simply asking questions" to get people to think more carefully about commonly accepted knowledge. People should be skeptical of any meme, video, or person that makes broad claims without providing any evidence to back them up, especially if the source claims that people who disagree with them are trying to silence them. Scientists such as Milo Rossi, who goes by Miniminuteman on YouTube, are committed to debunking archaeological conspiracy theories and spreading truth instead of lies.

Teotihuacán was built throughout the late first millennium BCE and early first millennium CE.

The Pyramid of the Sun consists of six stepped levels rising from a square base. The base is about 720 by 760 feet (220 m by 230 m) long, and the structure rises to a height of 216 feet (66 m). Tourists who visit the site today can climb to the top via a grand staircase located in the front.

The Pyramid of the Sun had a strong influence on later Mesoamerican peoples, including the Toltec, Maya, and Aztec peoples. Its features were reproduced "in countless variations of size, shape, and proportion throughout central Mexico," architectural historian Frederick Hartt wrote. "Its form became sharply steeper and higher in the Mayan civilization."[14] These great brick and stone pyramids demonstrate that Mesoamerican architecture was as large-scale and ambitious as what was created in Europe during the same period.

There are many other pyramids in Mexico. Shown here is the temple complex at Chichén Itzá.

CHAPTER THREE

THE GREEKS AND ROMANS

Many aspects of modern Western civilization are built on the ancient Greek and Roman cultures, which were very similar to each other. This includes architectural designs. After falling into a period of ruin, the Greeks spent their time and money rebuilding what they had lost and trying to get back to a more sustainable civilization. This effort brought Greece into what is known as the Archaic Age, which spanned from about 750 to 500 BCE. During this period, Greek city-states flourished, and people began adapting to new technologies and sciences in a way that changed the architecture world drastically. They began building temples out of stone, which was more durable than the mud-brick and wood that previous temples had been made of.

As these city-states progressed, they entered what became known as the Classical Age. This period of time, which lasted from about 500 to 323 BCE, was when the Greeks developed a political system that changed the way nations were run for centuries to come. Athens, one of the most powerful Greek city-states, created the first democracy. This opened up many new opportunities for civilization, and in turn, many new uses for buildings. For some time, architecture served few purposes: a place to live, a place to worship, or a place for communal gatherings. As societies became more complex, they needed buildings that served more specific purposes, which created new opportunities for architects.

In the late Archaic Age and early Classical Age, magnificent stone temples sprang up in Greece and in cities across the

Mediterranean world that were controlled by Greece. Along with these temples, the Greeks designed and built many new and original architectural masterpieces, including the world's first theaters.

Throughout these years, Greek culture, including architectural styles and elements, delighted and profoundly influenced other European cultures. In particular, the Romans, whose culture arose in Italy in the early first millennium BCE, absorbed the basics of Greek architecture. While the Greeks were artistically innovative, the Romans were more ambitious in terms of architectural engineering. As a result, Roman civilization applied architectural ideas borrowed from the Greeks in ways that suited Rome's individual needs and did so on a larger scale than the world had yet seen. Another crucial Roman achievement was to preserve Greece's artistic legacy and pass it on to later Europeans, who, in turn, passed it along to the rest of the world. The Greco-Roman style, also known as the classical tradition, became the strongest single force in later world architecture.

CLASSIC TEMPLES

The reason that classical Greek architecture developed around the temple was that for the Greeks, like the Egyptians, religion was an important part of daily life. During the Dark Age, before the Greeks became prosperous again, a common polytheistic religion—one that worshipped many gods—spread across the Greek lands. The most important god was Zeus, the god of the sky and ruler of the other gods and goddesses. The Greeks worshipped the same gods overall, but each individual city-state had its own patron god or goddess. The patron of Athens, for instance, was Athena, goddess of war and wisdom. It was thought that Athena protected and frequently visited the community and therefore required a place to stay there. For this reason, temples were the first form of monumental architecture that developed in post-Dark Age Greece. The Greeks spent huge amounts of time, resources, and energy on making temples as beautiful as possible. The Greeks believed the temple was an ideal architectural form because it honored and served the gods. Neal pointed out,

> *The philosophy behind Greek architecture was to discover the eternally valid rules that dictate form and proportion; to construct buildings of human scale that were suited to the divinity of their gods; Classical Greek architecture is [therefore] "ideal architecture." [It is no wonder] that elements of the style have been copied for over 2,500 years.*[15]

The earliest Greek temples were small, simple, hut-like structures made mostly of wood. They featured a front porch with a triangular pediment (the gable formed by the slanted roof), supported by two or four thin wooden columns. As the Archaic Age progressed, these structures quickly increased in size, complexity, and splendor. Builders added more columns, eventually forming a full colonnade (row of columns) that stretched around the whole building. The first known temple in this style was built on the Aegean island of Samos in the early 500s BCE. Dedicated to Hera, Zeus's wife, it was about 290 feet (88 m) long, was 150 feet (46 m) wide, and had a colonnade featuring more than 100 wooden columns. This temple became an example that the Greeks used to model their architectural style. It featured a rectangular inner enclosure with a main room called a *cella*; a front and back porch, each with a row of columns; colonnades running down the sides; and a low-pitched roof forming a triangular pediment on each end.

These basic architectural elements remained more or less the same for ages to come. However, the materials used in constructing temples became stronger and more durable over time. The roofs, for example, were originally composed of wooden timbers and thatch (layers of dry vegetation such as reeds or straw). In late Archaic times, pottery roofing tiles replaced the wood and thatch. Because the tiles were heavy, it became necessary to replace the wooden columns supporting the roof with stronger stone versions. By the dawn of the Classical Age, the changeover to all-stone temples was complete almost everywhere in Greece.

ARCHITECTURAL ORDERS

The late Archaic Age also witnessed the widespread adoption of two styles of architectural decoration, called orders. Temples on the Greek mainland mainly used the Doric order. Their columns stood directly on the temple floor without any sort of decorative base, and the column tops, or capitals, consisted of a rounded stone "cushion" resting under a flat stone slab. Doric buildings also featured a frieze, which is a decorative painted or sculpted band running horizontally above the colonnade. Doric friezes were not continuous; they were divided into separate rectangular elements, or panels, called metopes.

Another popular architectural order became dominant in the Aegean islands and in western Anatolia. This architectural decoration was known as the Ionic order because at the time, that region of Greece was called Ionia. Ionic columns had decorative bases, and their capitals featured elegant carved spirals called volutes. Another distinctive aspect of the Ionic style was the nature of its frieze. Rather than a series of separate panels, the frieze formed a continuous band above the colonnade. A third order, the Corinthian, developed much later and was used more by the Romans than the Greeks. The capitals of Corinthian columns were decorated with carved leaves and scrolls. The leaf carvings were typically arranged in three rows, with an elaborately carved flower resting at the top.

Sometimes Greek architects mixed various elements of the Doric and Ionic orders. An outstanding example of this is the Parthenon, a temple of Athena built on Athens's central hill, the Acropolis, in the fifth century BCE. It featured two friezes. A standard outward-facing Doric frieze graced the area above the colonnade. Meanwhile, a magnificent Ionic frieze containing hundreds of sculptured human and animal figures ran around the border on the inside of the colonnade. The reason for this extra and expensive decoration was that the Parthenon's designers, the architect Ictinus and sculptor

Pictured here from left to right are Ionic, Doric, and Corinthian style columns.

Phidias, conceived it on a grander scale than most other Greek temples. It originally contained 22,000 tons (19,800 mt) of marble. Today, it stands about 45 feet (14 m) tall, but because it is missing much of its roof, archaeologists can tell that it was even taller when it was originally built. Its larger-than-life sculpted figures of people and gods filled the open spaces within the pediments. A gold and ivory statue of Athena was created for the center interior of the structure.

In the fifth century CE, the Parthenon was converted into a Christian church. To do this, the renovators deliberately damaged or removed some of the friezes so they could block the east entrance (At the time, churches were traditionally entered from the west.) and put windows in the walls. In 1458, the Turks overtook the location and repurposed the structure as a mosque, adding a minaret—a tall, tower-like structure that is a feature of mosques—to the outside of the Parthenon. In 1687, most of the Parthenon was destroyed in an explosion during a battle between the Turks and the Venetians. The Venetians fired cannons at the building, damaging the exterior, and eventually, gunpowder that the Turks had stored inside the Parthenon caught fire and exploded, blowing out some of the exterior and much of the interior.

Restoration efforts started in 1983 so visitors could eventually see the Parthenon as it was originally built. Some of the sculptures and artifacts that were recovered over the years rest in the Louvre Museum in Paris and the British Museum in London. The Parthenon has inspired awe in those who have seen it throughout the ages. In 2017, architects voted it the most perfect building in the world in a poll conducted by *Business Insider*. Much of this opinion may be due to the fact that both the architect and sculptor who initially created the Parthenon worked in harmony to create a structure that was both functional and beautiful. It is this concept that still holds true in today's architectural ideologies.

PLACES TO GATHER

The Greeks applied elements of temple architecture, including the Doric and Ionic orders, to other public buildings.

Among these were treasuries, or small, ornately decorated structures for storing gold and other valuables. In fact, Greek treasuries looked like miniature versions of temples. Greek fountain houses were small buildings that held supplies of fresh water, which also looked like miniature temples. In addition, every Greek city-state had at least one town hall-like structure where local officials met and public banquets were staged. Such buildings were generally square, with rows of Doric or Ionic columns both outside and inside.

Another public structure common to Greek cities in the Classical Age and for centuries afterward was the theater. The Athenians invented both written plays and the institution of the theater in the late 500s BCE. Not long

THE ERECHTHEION

Resting near the remains of the Parthenon on Athens's Acropolis are the ruins of another temple dedicated to Athena and other gods—the Erechtheion. Some people believe the temple was the burial place of the mythical king Erechtheus. Another legend is that the temple was built after Athena and Poseidon, the Greek god of the oceans, competed to see who would be the city's patron. Poseidon hit the ground with his trident to make water flow out of the ground, while Athena hit the ground to make an olive tree grow. Because olives were an important part of the Greeks' diet, Athena won. The eastern part of the Erechtheion was dedicated to her, and she became the city's patron, or main goddess.

Architecturally speaking, the Erechtheion followed a plan that was quite unusual for Greek temples of that time. It had two porches, one each on its north and south sides, all set in an asymmetrical, split-level arrangement to account for the slant of the land it was placed upon. The south-facing porch came to be called the "Porch of the Maidens" because its roof is supported by six caryatids—pillars shaped like maidens wearing flowing robes. The temple also had unusual openings in the floor so people could see the marks the Greeks believed were left by Poseidon's trident when he hit the ground during his contest with Athena.

A caryatid is a column that is carved to look like a woman.

afterward, the Athenians constructed the Theater of Dionysus at the foot of the Acropolis. It consisted of a circular orchestra, or "dancing place," where the actors performed, and a semicircular audience area that eventually sat up to 14,000 people. A rectangular structure called the *skene*, or "scene building," was put up behind the orchestra. The skene provided a background for the actors and also housed dressing rooms and perhaps a storage area for stage props.

Although religious temples were the main examples of monumental architecture in ancient Greece, the Greeks did produce some large-scale nonreligious architecture, too. One of the most common and beautiful examples was the stoa. Built most often in marketplaces, it was a long rectangular structure with an open walkway running along the front. The overhanging roof of the walkway was supported by a row of Doric or Ionic columns. To the rear of this open-air corridor were several small chambers used as workrooms and merchants' stalls. The roofed walkways of stoas were places for people to find shelter from the sun and rain. Over time, they also became meeting places, where informal political and philosophical discussions and educational lectures took place.

SIMILARITIES AND DIFFERENCES

In a number of ways, Roman architecture, especially that of temples, looked similar to Greek architecture. This is not surprising, since the Romans borrowed most of their design elements from Greek architecture. There were, however, significant differences between the architectural traditions and achievements of the two peoples. Over the course of several centuries, the Romans created a huge empire with a largely efficient centralized government, a feat the Greeks never managed. The needs of the empire demanded new kinds of public structures that were both practical and large scale. "The complexities and importance of large-scale commerce," one expert observer noted,

The Roman Empire covered far more than modern-day Italy. This Roman colosseum in Tunisia is the largest in North Africa.

called for open, large-scale interior spaces that could be enlivened by the hustle and bustle of much human traffic and activity. Law courts needed impressive, high-ceilinged chambers; extensive, many-chambered, roofed-over spaces were needed for … such popular diversions as the public baths; vast amphitheaters and arenas were needed for entertaining the tax-paying populace.[16]

The Roman amphitheaters were huge, oval-shaped stadiums for staging wild animal shows and fights between gladiators. The biggest and most famous was the Colosseum in Rome. Its oval bowl measures about 615 by 512 feet (188 by 156 m) in width and more than 156 feet (47 m) in height. The seats are no longer intact, so the exact seating capacity is uncertain. However, most modern experts agree that the Colosseum held some 50,000 spectators. It fell into ruin because of earthquakes and because medieval Romans used the stones to build other things.

Even larger than amphitheaters were facilities called circuses, where the Romans held chariot races. They were called circuses because they were round, and *circus* is the Latin word for "circle." In each circus, huge stone seating sections surrounded a dirt racetrack with a long, narrow barrier—the *euripus*—running down the middle. The euripus was crowded with statues, altars, pillars, and other decorative elements. In each race, the charioteers drove their teams 7 times around the euripus, a distance of roughly 3 miles (4.8 km). The largest and most famous Roman circus was the Circus Maximus in the city of Rome. It was some 2,000 feet (610 m) long, 600 feet (190 m) wide, and made to fit more than 250,000 people.

In addition to large-scale facilities for entertainment, the Romans also built basilicas—huge public structures used for political meetings, law courts, and various administrative and social functions. Architecturally speaking, a basilica consisted of a large open central space, called the nave, with large aisles running down its sides. High above the nave was a vaulted roof, and outside each entrance was a covered porch lined with columns. Basilicas turned out to be one of the most important Roman contributions to world architecture because over time, their form became the basis for many early Christian churches. However, Catholics today do not use the term "basilica" to refer to a church's architecture; for them, it means a church that has been given special status by the pope.

Today, the Circus Maximus (shown here) is a public park.

THE ROMAN STYLE

Basilicas, amphitheaters, and most other Roman architectural forms consistently used certain architectural elements and construction materials that became Roman trademarks. Among the more familiar are the arch and vault. A Roman arch featured two vertical stone piers topped by a semicircle composed of wedge-shaped stones called voussoirs. The central and topmost voussoir was called the keystone. A Roman vault was essentially an arch carried into three dimensions—a curved ceiling. If such a ceiling ran down the length of the corridor, it was called a barrel vault, a common feature of the corridors of both theaters and amphitheaters in Roman lands.

AN IMPORTANT ESSAY

In medieval and modern times, the best-known ancient Roman architect was Marcus Vitruvius Pollio, most often referred to simply as Vitruvius. His fame rested mainly on his essay—written in the 20s BCE—titled *De Architectura*, Latin for *On Architecture*. The work covers all kinds of Greek and Roman building, along with related topics including common building materials, mathematics, civil engineering, town planning, the architectural orders, aqueducts, mechanical devices, and more. After Rome's fall, a few handwritten copies of the book survived. In 1486, the first published edition became a sensation among European architects and intellectuals. Little is known about Vitruvius's life beyond the fact that he was a practicing Roman architect and engineer from about 46 to 30 BCE.

In the third century BCE, the Romans found that adding a special kind of volcanic sand to lime in a specific ratio produced concrete, which is a remarkably hard, strong, and durable substance. The use of concrete in addition to marble, granite, wood, and other traditional materials became a trademark of Roman architecture. Another advantage of this material was that it hardened underwater, making it ideal for building bridges over rivers. Constituting another of Rome's great achievements in monumental architecture, some of these bridges were so sturdy that they are still in use today and easily carry the weight of cars and trucks.

The features of Greco-Roman architecture survived longer than the ancient Greek and Roman societies did. Over time, these features were used in other buildings around the world. Even today, modern buildings such as banks, museums, and government buildings use columns, pediments, and other Greco-Roman features. The White House, where the United States president lives, is an example of a modern structure built in the Roman style.

The architects of the White House took inspiration from Greek and Roman buildings.

CHAPTER FOUR

MEDIEVAL ARCHITECTURE

Over time, architectural tastes have changed. Many people fiercely debate which buildings are the most beautiful and useful. The answer is a matter of personal opinion, but there is a clear difference between ancient (or ancient-inspired) and modern architecture. What is known today as the medieval era or Middle Ages was a time when many drastic changes in architecture took place. This period lasted from around 476 CE to 1300. Many historians believe that this time period was the turning point from what is now considered ancient times to what is now considered modern times.

During this time period, as in periods that came before it, much of the architecture was formed around religious worship. Temples were advancing, but stupas continued to be something of a guide for future religious structures in Asia to follow. In Europe, however, different religions began to develop, and many had their own style of architecture for their buildings of worship. The Roman emperor Constantine made Christianity the national religion after he unified Rome in 324 CE. As a result, thousands of churches and cathedrals were constructed across Europe.

CASTLE ARCHITECTURE

Along with churches, castles were the architectural trademarks of medieval Europe. Not only architecturally, but also militarily and socially, castles dominated the lives of medieval Europeans, especially after the year 1000. They housed the continent's kings, lords, and other nobles and became the main local and regional centers of food distribution, tax collection, political and legal decision-making, and warfare. In these ways, the masters of castles exerted control over the thousands of ordinary people who lived in surrounding farms and villages.

The basic architectural concepts that went into the creation of the first castles in Europe were not new. Large fortresses had been common in the Middle East for thousands of years, and the ancient Romans had built massive forts across many parts of Europe. Medieval European builders began creating primitive castles in northern France in the late 9th and early 10th centuries, and the idea quickly spread to Germany and other neighboring lands. Made mainly of wood, these structures became known as motte and bailey castles. A motte was a low hill on which the builders constructed a wooden barrier. Below the motte and also protected by a barrier were one or more baileys—courtyards in which people as well as domestic animals could find protection when enemies threatened the territory.

A new and larger phase of castle building began in the 11th century. The older wooden enclosures were replaced with sturdier, more durable stone walls. The result was a structure called a shell keep. It consisted of a circular stone wall enclosing a wide courtyard, which contained workshops, stables, and small living quarters. The tops of the walls featured an idea borrowed from ancient Middle Eastern fortresses—crenellation. Crenellation consisted of alternating stone notches and open spaces; during an attack, soldiers hid behind the notches and fired arrows through the open spaces. Simple shell keeps quickly developed into larger, more complex structures with taller, thicker walls and stone living quarters in the centers of the courtyards. The largest single room was generally called the "hall" and served as both a meeting area and a dining room for the castle's residents.

Meanwhile, weapons technology was advancing, making sieges of castles more successful. In response, the outer defenses—or battlements—of European castles became increasingly more resistant to attack. "It was the serious affair of every great leader," historian Sidney Toy wrote, "to be familiar with the latest methods of attack and defence, since his safety and the safety of his followers depended upon his ability to [repel an] assault."[17] To this end, builders added such features as tall, crenellated guard towers, machicolation, and the portcullis. Machicolation consisted of the outward slant of a wall at the top of the battlements. Missiles or boiling oil could be dropped onto attackers through openings in the floors of these projections. A portcullis was a heavy gateway door constructed of thick wood reinforced with iron plates. Defenders could move it up and down using chains

Crennellation (also called battlements) and towers are two iconic parts of castles.

attached to a pulley operated from a small chamber above the main gate.

Many European castles also had a drawbridge in front of the portcullis. A drawbridge was a wooden platform that generally rested in a horizontal position over the protective moat (a wide pit, typically filled with water) that was a feature of most castles. During an attack, the defenders pulled the drawbridge upward, using chains attached to the outer ends of the bridge, until the bridge stood upright against the front of the portcullis.

One of the most imposing and best-preserved of Europe's medieval castles—Château de Vincennes—displays all of these classic features of castle architecture. Located not far east of Paris, France, the structure dates from 1150, with major additions completed in the early 1400s. The chateau's towering stone defensive walls, equipped with impressive machicolation, stretch for more than 0.5 mile (1 km) and have six guard towers and three huge gates. The largest of all is a massive stone tower situated inside the courtyard; the tallest fortified structure built in medieval Europe, it rises to a height of 170 feet (52 m).

CHRISTIAN INFLUENCES

Even as the first castles were sprouting up across Europe in early medieval times, monumental religious architecture was already evident in some places. In Rome's final century or so, Christians gained control of the Roman government. In the years following the empire's disintegration, Christianity became the dominant faith of Europe. Therefore, in most parts of medieval Europe, religious architecture consisted of Christian churches and cathedrals.

Even before Rome's fall, Christians were building large churches. Initially, for the sake of convenience, they took over and refurbished existing Roman basilicas. This made sense from a logistical standpoint, since basilicas were big meeting places that could accommodate large numbers of people. As time went on and new churches were built from scratch, the basic basilica form continued to be used. Certain changes were made, however. The nave, which is the large central area of the church, is where all the services are held. In the back of the nave is the apse, which is a semicircular recess where the altar is placed. Architectural innovations also added a transept, which is a rectangular space crossing the nave at a right angle in front of the altar. Thereby, the nave and transept together formed a basic cross, further symbolizing the Christian faith.

An example of early Christian architecture is Hagia Sophia, an enormous church (now mosque) in what is now Istanbul. After the fall of the western part of the Roman Empire, the eastern part grew into the Byzantine Empire. Byzantine Christian churches also used the basilica form, but they displayed many new refinements. One of the most noticeable changes was a huge dome soaring directly above the nave. Hagia Sophia's dome is about 108 feet (33 m) across and 180 feet (55 m) tall, and it rests on four columns. This architectural configuration—a dome placed atop a group of columns lining a square-shaped hall—became the most familiar trademark of Byzantine architecture. Even further, this configuration became somewhat of a staple in cathedral architecture around the world for years to come. It produced a central interior space of great majesty, beauty, and spiritual inspiration.

On seeing the completed Hagia Sophia, the early Byzantine historian Procopius remarked,

> *The church has been made a spectacle of great beauty, stupendous to those who see it … In the middle of the church there rise four [giant columns] … Upon these are placed four arches so as to form a square … Above the arches, the construction rises in a circle [above which] is an enormous spherical dome which makes the building exceptionally beautiful. It seems not to be founded on solid masonry, but to be suspended from heaven.*[18]

Hagia Sophia is considered one of the most beautiful buildings in the world.

GOTHIC CATHEDRALS

The first European cathedral created fully in the Gothic style was the Basilica of Saint Denis in Paris, completed in 1144. Its Gothic spires, stained glass windows, and other architectural elements were conceived to glorify God. The nave is supported by 12 columns, corresponding to the 12 apostles, with just as many in the aisles, corresponding to the 12 prophets.

Saint Denis is one of the earliest examples of Gothic architecture. As time went on, the Gothic style evolved into what came to be called High Gothic. High Gothic cathedrals were generally larger and more elaborate, with bigger stained glass windows. These let in more light and color, giving cathedrals an airy feel rather than a dark and gloomy one.

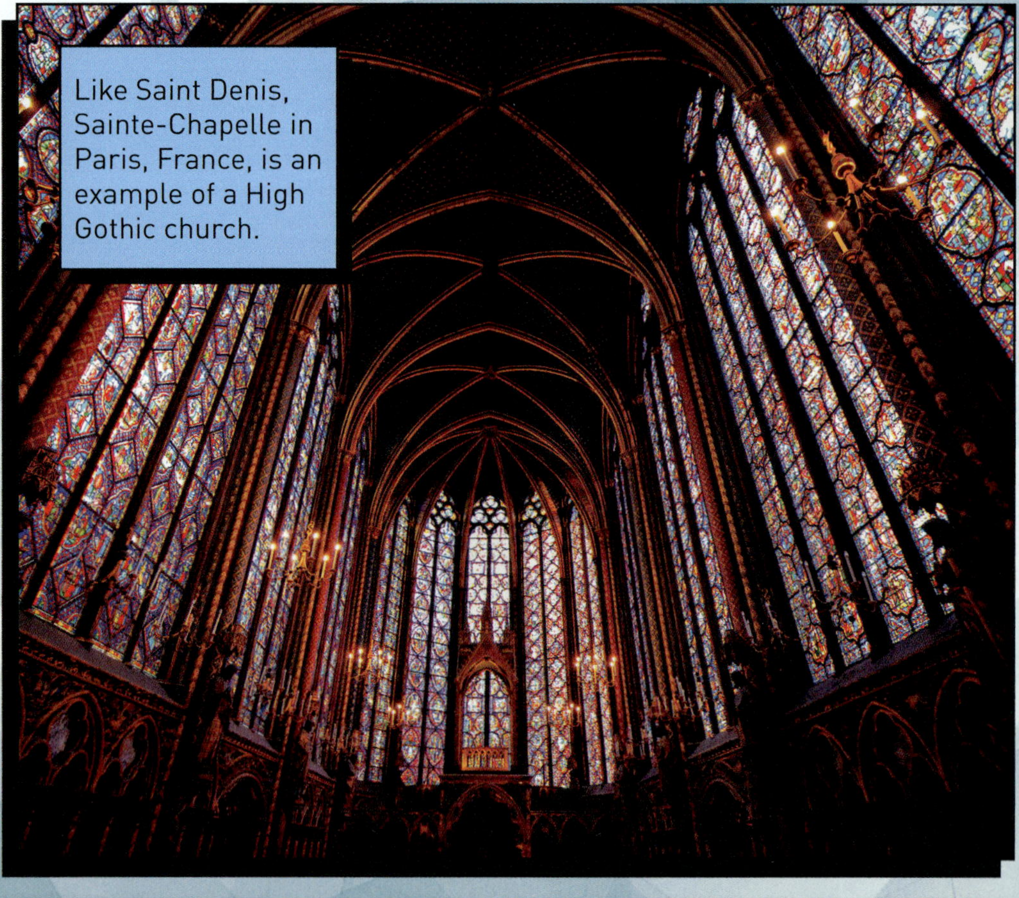

Like Saint Denis, Sainte-Chapelle in Paris, France, is an example of a High Gothic church.

Notre-Dame Cathedral in Paris, France, is an example of an Early Gothic church.

THE RISE OF THE GOTHIC STYLE

The Romanesque period of art and architecture, which began around the year 1000, was characterized partly by the resemblance of the new churches to older Roman buildings. In particular, huge, rectangular blocks of stone and rounded arches, both trademarks of Roman construction, were in wide use. However, the main differences between Romanesque structures and those that preceded them were size and ornamentation. The new churches were both larger and more highly decorated than earlier churches. "Interior surfaces were covered with wall paintings," architectural historian Michael Raeburn pointed out. "Porches, columns, [and] whole facades were decorated with sculpture and then painted, too."[19]

Shortly after CE 1120, Europe's Romanesque style began to give way to an even more imposing style that later came to be called Gothic. Gothic churches first appeared in France in the 12th century and continued to be built in Europe for several centuries, even after the introduction of newer styles. Among the key differences between Romanesque and Gothic architecture are that Gothic added height, lightness of form, and large glass windows to let in more light. As noted architectural historians H.W. Janson and Anthony F. Janson put it: "The [Gothic] architectural forms seem graceful, almost weightless, compared to the massive solidity of the Romanesque. In addition, the windows have been enlarged to the point that they are no longer openings cut into a wall—they themselves become translucent walls."[20]

Flying buttresses help support the heavy walls of large stone buildings.

TAILORED TO THE AREA

The place where a building is constructed has a huge influence on what that building looks like. Climate is one very important factor an architect must consider when designing a building. Bjarke Ingels, a Danish architect, gave several examples of how buildings have been shaped by their surroundings:

> *There is a reason the hillsides of Santorini and other Greek islands are speckled with Cubist whitewashed homes. The white color reflects heat, and the flat roofs make for cool, breezy retreats in the evening ... . And in some villages in Yemen, buildings have peculiar chimneys that collect wind to create natural ventilation.*[1]

Ingels added that as technology has advanced, there is sometimes less need for these kinds of considerations. For example, after the invention of air conditioning, architects did not need to be as concerned about which way a building faced to collect the most breeze. Technology has allowed modern architects to design buildings in ways previous cultures could not.

1. Megan Gambino, "Designing Buildings For Hot Climates, Cold Ones and Everything in Between," *Smithsonian*, February 5, 2015. www.smithsonianmag.com/innovation/designing-buildings-for-hot-climates-cold-ones-and-everything-in-between-180954003/.

Another trademark of Gothic architecture is the flying buttress. Because Gothic cathedrals, such as Notre-Dame in Paris, are so tall and broad, the immense weight of their upper sections pushes outward toward the sides. To counter this effect and thereby keep the building from falling down, medieval builders developed the flying buttress. This stone structure, engineering expert L. Sprague de Camp explained, is "like a small section of an arch, leaning against the piers from outside the building, propping up the wall and counterbalancing the thrust of the roof vault."[21] Notre-Dame was one of the first European cathedrals to utilize flying buttresses. They help hold up the walls and roof of the nave, which are an impressive 115 feet (35 m) high.

MOSQUE FEATURES

In the early centuries of Europe's medieval period, well before the Notre-Dame Cathedral was built, Muslim armies conquered much of the Middle East, North Africa, and southern Spain.

The Muslims not only introduced their religion, Islam, to these regions; they also developed religious architecture used mainly in Islamic churches, which are called mosques. The Islamic architectural style was in many ways distinct from European styles. Muslim builders adopted architectural elements and ideas from various peoples, especially the Persians, Romans, Egyptians, and Byzantines. The Roman arch and the Byzantine dome, for example, were incorporated into numerous Islamic structures. The result was a unique and elegant composite architectural approach.

Religious beliefs influence the way religious buildings are designed. Mosques have several architectural features that are not found in churches or other buildings. These features are specific to the ways Muslims worship God, or Allah. For instance, when Muslims pray, they face the direction of Mecca, the city where the prophet Muhammad was born. For this reason, mosques have a mihrab, which is an alcove in the wall that shows which direction Mecca is. The location of the mihrab inside a mosque varies depending on which direction Mecca lies from that mosque; for example, a mihrab in an Indian mosque will be on the west wall, while one in an Egyptian mosque will be on the east wall. The wall containing the mihrab is called the *qibla* wall. (*Qibla* is the word for the direction of Mecca).

Mosques also typically feature a minaret, which is a tall tower where the call to prayer is announced. Because minarets are easily recognizable and are associated only with mosques, they also remind everyone who sees them of Islam. The minaret is important because it reminds Muslims of their faith.

Some mosques have features that are determined more by climate and geography than religion. For example, many mosques feature a *sahn*, which is an open courtyard attached to the main prayer hall. Since Islam has its roots in countries with warm climates, many sahns have a fountain in them that was originally intended to cool people down and give them somewhere to do the washing that is required before they pray. Mosques built in places with cold weather may not have a sahn. Similarly, domes are not a requirement for religious worship, but many mosques have them because Muslim architects were influenced by the Byzantines; they liked the way the domes looked, so they used them in their own buildings. For Muslims, the dome came to symbolize heaven, so although it may not originally have had significance, it does today. The placement of the dome also has religious meaning. Some mosques have multiple domes, while others only have one. When only one dome is present, it is placed over the qibla wall because that is considered to be the holiest spot in the mosque.

Today, mosques can be found all over the world, but there were few, if any, mosques in northern Europe until the 1800s. The structures that were being built in most of Europe changed as the continent progressed from the medieval period to what historians call the Renaissance.

Most people who live in Dubai in the United Arab Emirates are Muslim. For this reason, Dubai has many stunning mosques, including the Sharjah Grand Mosque (shown here).

CHAPTER FIVE

THE RENAISSANCE PERIOD

In Europe, during the final stretch of the medieval era and into the period referred to as the Renaissance, huge strides were taken to improve architecture and its practices. The Renaissance lasted from around 1300 CE to 1600 CE. The biggest difference between this time period compared to the others was that it expanded upon previous innovations, creating a more accurate and "perfect" means of constructing a building. The term "renaissance" means "rebirth" and was used because this time period improved on many ideas from previous civilizations. Ancient Rome was an especially important influence on Renaissance architecture.

MATH IN ARCHITECTURE

The biggest advancement in Renaissance architecture is the proportioned, symmetrical interior spaces based on mathematics. Math has always been an important part of architecture, even in early civilizations, because if a building's measurements are not precise, the building will not hold up for long. However, Renaissance architects used math to determine not just the functionality of the building, but the form as well. They used geometry—a branch of mathematics that deals with lines and shapes—to achieve a harmonious flow of structures by converting numbered ratios into physical spaces. For example, exterior walls would be symmetrical in the sense that each measurement was the same as or half of the previous number. These measurements were considered to be perfect, which is why they were believed to bring worshippers closer to God. Neal wrote, "The rediscovery of one of Pythagoras's theories—that musical intervals in harmony were exactly proportional to numbers in physical dimensions—gave architects a basis for proportions, linking music and architecture via mathematics."[22] It was believed that through this theory, architecture became closer to nature.

This attention to harmony, proportion, and mathematics could be seen in the way architects drew the plans for their buildings. They used perspective—a mathematical way to draw objects in space—to give a more accurate view of how the buildings would look when they were built. The sizes and placement of doors, windows, stairways, terraces, balustrades, columns, and other architectural elements were chosen to make their buildings look more interesting and beautiful.

Renaissance architects strongly emphasized several elements, including frequent use of Greco-Roman pediments, or variations of them, on the fronts of buildings. Doric, Ionic, and Corinthian columns were also common elements of both the exteriors and interiors of Renaissance buildings. Most often, such columns were load-bearing, meaning they supported upper stories or roofs. However, Renaissance architecture also made widespread use of pilasters—non-load-bearing, flattened or shortened columns attached to outer or inner walls mainly for decoration. Renaissance interiors also featured decorative effects such as frescoes—paintings done on wet plaster—and richly detailed moldings. In addition, domes, based on Roman models, became popular for the exteriors of Renaissance buildings. Renaissance builders used all of these architectural elements not only for churches, but also for structures such as palaces, private villas, libraries, hospitals, and other types of public buildings. Much like the temples in ancient Greece, several different people with different skill sets came together to create a structure. This diversity in skill helped tie in each element of a building to further perfect its overall appearance and function.

FLORENCE CATHEDRAL

The special requirements of the dome of the Basilica of Saint Mary of the Flower—also known simply as Florence Cathedral—inspired the first significant architectural achievement of the Renaissance. The events in question took place in the city-state of Florence, in north-central Italy, which became the initial focus of architectural activity in this period. By the late 1300s, Florence had become a major European center of learning as well as a military power that competed for political dominance with other Italian states. To increase their prestige, the Florentines poured large sums of money into large-scale construction projects, including the Basilica of Saint Mary.

Work on the basilica had begun in the late 1200s and continued off and on for more than a century. By 1418, all that was left to build was the dome. According to the design, it had to be 137 feet (42 m) wide at the base. The problem was that no one in Europe had built such an enormous dome during the previous 900 years, and local architects were uncertain as to how to go about it. If the dome was too heavy, it would crush the building. The government therefore held a contest for the best design. The winner was Filippo Brunelleschi, who turned out to be the first great architect of the Renaissance.

In tackling this challenge, Brunelleschi drew inspiration mainly from the great dome of the ancient Pantheon in Rome, which was still in use in the 15th century (and remains in excellent condition today). Brunelleschi observed that one reason that the Pantheon's dome had remained intact for so many centuries was that the builders had coffered the stones making up its bulk. Coffering means they had partly hollowed out each stone to reduce the dome's overall weight.

To achieve even more weight reduction in his own dome, Brunelleschi made a design featuring two relatively thin domes made of stone and brick, one covering the other. A series of iron and stone ribs connect the inner dome to the outer one, leaving mostly empty space between. In this brilliant arrangement, the domes reinforce each other, while the ribs carry most of their weight downward onto eight

Domes can come in various shapes and sizes. This style is called an onion dome.

THE DOME OF THE PANTHEON

Located in Rome, Italy, the Pantheon served as a temple to honor the Roman gods during the reign of Augustus. The temple has been rebuilt multiple times, most of which were for renovation and preservation purposes. The dome on the inside of the massive structure is the largest concrete dome created without alternative reinforcements. Much was, and can still be, learned about construction processes and possibilities in architecture from this building.

The dome of the Pantheon is considered an architectural marvel.

Florence Cathedral also has an impressive dome.

massive piers embedded in the walls below the dome. Even factoring in the weight reduction afforded by the design, the combined domes are still phenomenally heavy at 40,785 tons (37,000 mt).

Brunelleschi completed the dome in 1436. During the construction process, he invented several special hoisting machines to lift the materials high above the cathedral floor. These became models for hoists used by builders across Europe during the Renaissance. Brunelleschi himself used them on his own later buildings. Among the more influential of these was another church—San Lorenzo (the Basilica of Saint Lawrence), also in Florence. Work began on it in the 1420s while Saint Mary's great dome was still under construction. The general floor plans of San Lorenzo and some other Florentine churches Brunelleschi designed were widely copied throughout Europe in the centuries that followed.

MICHELANGELO'S CONTRIBUTIONS

In certain ways, the great Italian artist, sculptor, and architect Michelangelo di Lodovico Buonarroti continued the architectural styles and ideas developed by Brunelleschi and other earlier Renaissance masters. For example, one of the great facades Michelangelo created in the splendid town square he designed, the Campidoglio, resembles the front of Leon Battista Alberti's Palazzo Rucellai, which took inspiration from the Roman Colosseum. Work on the Campidoglio, at the summit of Rome's Capitoline Hill, began in the 1540s. Although both it and the Palazzo Rucellai include pilasters and arches, Michelangelo's are much larger, so the Campidoglio looks more dramatic than the Palazzo Rucellai.

Another architectural achievement by Michelangelo was the dome, or cupola, of Saint Peter's Basilica in Rome. Though Michelangelo designed the dome, at the time of his death in 1564, only its supports had been constructed. Additions to the design were made between 1585 and 1590 by architect Giacomo della Porta and engineer Domenico Fontana. The finished product was a double dome like the one Brunelleschi created.

The diameter of Saint Peter's dome's interior space is 139 feet (42.5 m), and its highest interior point soars an amazing 394 feet (120 m) above the floor. This famous structure became the inspiration for many large domes built later across the globe, notably those of Saint Paul's Cathedral in London and the U.S. Capitol in Washington, D.C.

The Sistine Chapel is among the most widely known architectural masterpieces. It is also accompanied by one of the most important pieces of art history. Created in Vatican City, the chapel is 132 feet (40.23 m) long, 44 feet (13.4 m) wide, and 68 feet (20.7 m) tall. Though Michelangelo did not design the building, he was commissioned to use his talents elsewhere in the chapel to paint frescoes on the ceiling. This exhausting task took him four years. The most famous of the frescoes, titled *The Creation of Adam*, is an imagined scene from Genesis, the first book of the Bible. This scene shows God breathing life into Adam, the first man. This painting, present in one of the most

The Sistine Chapel features beautiful paintings on its ceiling.

ARCHITECTURE FAILS

Everyone makes mistakes—even architects. One famous example is Fidenae Stadium, which was built in 27 CE in the town of Fidenae, near Rome. The architect, a man named Atilius, wanted to build a large amphitheater quickly and cheaply, on ground that was not solid enough to support it. As a result, it was poorly constructed and used flimsy materials. During the first event to be held there, the stadium collapsed, killing about 50,000 people. The Roman Senate quickly passed a law forbidding the construction of buildings on uncertain ground—one of the first building codes in history.

Architectural failures are not confined to the past. A modern example is 20 Fenchurch Street in London, England. At first, the building was nicknamed the "Walkie Talkie" because of its unusual shape. Later, however, it earned the unfortunate nickname of "the Fryscraper." The building's shape and its glass-covered exterior reflect sunlight so strongly in some spots that the temperature can reach over 242 degrees Fahrenheit (117 degrees Celsius). These hot spots have melted cars parked nearby and set neighboring stores on fire. To fix the problem, sunshade fins were installed on the front.

The Leaning Tower of Pisa is technically an architectural failure, but it is this failure that makes it so famous.

well-known chapels in the world, is a beautiful addition to the architectural functionality of the structure. It is also one of the most well-regarded and studied paintings in history.

Michelangelo's theatricality and innovative ideas are even more evident in the interior spaces he created for the Laurentian Library in Florence. The entrance hall leading to the main section of the library consists of a combination of classical architectural elements positioned in unclassical ways. The columns on either side of the door, for instance, are recessed into the wall instead of projected outward from it. Also, the pilasters on the walls are unevenly spaced and taper downward, something never seen in Greco-Roman versions. In addition, the central staircase leading to the door widens as it moves downward, and the stairs are of increasingly unequal widths and curved rather than rectangular. "Walking up or down this amazing structure," Frederick Hartt observed, "is an experience so disturbing as to leave little doubt that the harmonies … [of earlier Renaissance buildings] have been left far behind."[23]

Clearly, in shaping the interiors of the Laurentian Library and some of his other architectural works, Michelangelo was interested less in function and symmetry and more in expressing his individuality and creative side. For this reason, he is often categorized as a mannerist. Mannerism was a sub-period of Renaissance art lasting from about 1520 to 1600. Mannerists continued to use classical elements, as Michelangelo did in the library hall, but they tended to experiment more than their immediate predecessors. In so doing, their works were often more eclectic (mixing diverse ideas or styles), unusual, and theatrical, and they featured exaggerated or less harmonious proportions.

The Renaissance was a crucial period in the innovation of architecture around the world. The most important advancement was in the relationship between the functionality of the building itself and the beauty that accompanies it. For example, Michelangelo was, among other things, both an architect and a painter. His wide range of skill sets allowed him to bring several different ideas and perspectives to the table when creating a structure, both inside and out.

Mesa Verde is one of the largest cliff dwellings in what is now the United States.

AMERICAN PUEBLOS

Discussions about early architecture often focus on the achievements of the Europeans, but it is important to remember that non-European cultures were also developing their own styles of art and architecture at the same time. For instance, in Taos, New Mexico, the Tiwa people began building houses made out of a type of clay called adobe, which was widely available in their area.

The houses were all connected to each other, creating a pueblo, which is Spanish for "village." The entrances were on the roofs; people climbed in and out of their houses using ladders. The thick walls "kept the pueblos cool in summer and warm in winter. The roof was made of pine logs with earth placed on top, and the movable ladders prevented invading nomadic tribes from getting inside easily."[1] These pueblos eventually spread across the American Southwest because they were easy to build, especially in areas that had few other building materials, and had great benefits for the people who lived in them.

New Mexico is also the site of what is now Mesa Verde National Park, where visitors can climb up to the cliff dwellings made by the Anasazi people. Mesa Verde is not the only cliff pueblo, but it is unique because it is exceptionally large and well-preserved.

1. Giles Laroche, *If You Lived Here: Houses of the World*. Boston, MA: Houghton Mifflin Harcourt, 2011, p. 5.

Shown here is a pueblo.

The end results were some of the most extraordinary structures ever built. This is true of much of the architecture that emerged in the Renaissance: Both form and function were taken into consideration, creating a beautiful and useful masterpiece. To this day, several architectural monuments of the Renaissance period are still standing and remain some of the most well constructed, beautiful buildings in the world.

Many people come from around the world to appreciate the architecture of Rome.

CHAPTER SIX

LATER STYLES

The period after the Renaissance, roughly spanning the years 1600 to 1800, is referred to as the early modern period. During this period, several architectural styles were created, including the baroque and neoclassical styles. Each style differed in individual architectural elements, but a common factor of each was pulling ideas from previous periods and refining them to a more modern standpoint. Revival of old styles became a common practice in architecture. An interest in past architectural styles grew among cultures, and imitating their incredible structures became a common occurrence in each architectural masterpiece.

The early modern period borrowed heavily from elements of the Gothic style. What became known as Gothic revival was very prominent in the 19th century. This borrowing of ideas blended the Renaissance style with the Greco-Roman style. Even today, elements of each of these styles are sometimes adapted into architecture.

The early modern period of architecture spread around the world and continued to adapt according to each individual culture. Countries around the world began to evolve their architectural styles in order to adapt to new cultural situations.

BAROQUE

The first major architectural style of the early modern period was not a revival but a reworking of a style called mannerism. The new style, called "baroque," thrived from roughly 1600 to the early 1700s. Mannerist and baroque structures can appear very similar. The mannerists exaggerated many elements of Renaissance architecture, and in turn, baroque architects adapted and exaggerated elements of the mannerist style. On the whole, baroque architecture is characterized by extreme degrees of detail and ornamentation as well as an indulgence into personal expression by the architects. This style of architecture influenced other parts of European culture as well. Baroque "came to stand for anything that was elaborate and grandiose. Fashion and music also changed with the times. Bulging skirts and grand orchestras provided ideal accompaniment to the splendid new buildings."[24]

Baroque buildings often made sculptures and paintings nearly as prominent as standard architectural elements. Thus, the baroque period of art witnessed a sort of fusion, or combination, of the artistic disciplines of architecture, sculpture, and painting. A good example of this fusion, as well as the fusion between two architectural time periods, is Saint Peter's Basilica. Though it was initially created by Michelangelo in the 1500s, an architect named Gian Lorenzo Bernini revised some elements of the original architecture. The biggest revision was the addition of what is known as a piazza, or an outdoor public meeting place. This piazza was created by building several columns around the basilica, creating something similar to a town square in front of it.

Bernini continued on in the architectural world and became widely famous for his masterpiece—the Cornaro Chapel at Santa Maria della Vittoria in Rome, completed in 1652. As a sculptor and an architect, he, much like Michelangelo, combined both of his skill sets. This, in turn, prompted him to design an entire structure to house and show off the qualities of his magnificent sculpture, *The Ecstasy of Saint Theresa*. The ceiling is a great barrel vault covered with painted clouds, rays of sunlight, and flying angels. Far beneath, to the rear of the altar, the *Ecstasy* rests in a recessed niche surrounded by Corinthian columns and layer upon layer of ornately decorated moldings, as well as other architectural, sculptural, and painted details.

The Palace of Versailles is an example of baroque architecture. Shown here is the palace's famous Hall of Mirrors.

LESS ORNATE

In the baroque style, European architects refined and decorated Renaissance structures with so much attention to detail that there was simply no way to make them any more elaborate. With seemingly nowhere left to go in this direction, intense, ornamental detail took a backseat to classic, solidified architectural structure. In some ways, it can be seen as a reversal of direction or a return to the more basic and substantial classical architectural forms created during the Renaissance. Appropriately, the new period, or style, of architecture came to be called neoclassicism. ("Neo" is a prefix that means "new.") It lasted roughly from the mid-1700s to the early 1800s.

Neoclassical architects aimed to revive Greco-Roman themes and elements that were more simplified, while still keeping some detail from the baroque period. One of the cultural motivations for the outburst of neoclassical architecture was the discovery of Pompeii and Herculaneum in the

Palladian windows are still commonly used today even in otherwise ordinary buildings.

mid-1700s. These ancient Roman towns had been buried during a large volcanic eruption in the first century CE. Seeing the emerging ruins of the buried towns, European architects were inspired to recapture the glory of Greece and grandeur of Rome.

However, an even more powerful inspiration for neoclassical architects consisted of the works of the late Renaissance architect Andrea Palladio. The facades of his buildings had quite often featured a row of columns topped by a triangular pediment—an architectural form borrowed directly from the front porches of Greco-Roman temples. Another of Palladio's trademarks had been his windows. A Palladian window (sometimes also called a Venetian window) was topped by a Roman arch, was flanked by decorative pilasters, and generally had a balustrade projecting from the bottom. Neoclassical architects were inspired by Palladio's style, which used simplicity to create elegant buildings.

A POPULAR STYLE

Neoclassical buildings borrowing these and other classical architectural elements were built across large portions of Europe as well as the United States and other lands originally settled by Europeans. Such structures were particularly popular in England, where the style was first applied in a major way. The first outstanding example was Chiswick House near London, begun in 1725 and designed by Richard Boyle, better known as Lord Burlington. The house's front porch consists of a Palladian-style temple facade fronted by a row of six columns and topped by a pediment. Stairways with elegant handrails flow downward from each side of the porch; they are evenly spaced, as neoclassicism tried to revive the classical concept of symmetry that mannerist and baroque builders had often ignored. Behind the front porch, above the main section of the house, appears a simple dome with no decoration on it. Overall, the structure has a sense of balance and restraint almost never seen in baroque structures.

Though the distinctive look of Chiswick House's exterior was frequently reproduced (with some variations) in later neoclassical buildings, the architects of the era did not ignore the interiors of these structures. One of the finest examples of neoclassical interior design is the library for Kenwood House in London, completed in 1769. The architect was Robert Adam, widely seen as the dominant figure in European neoclassical architecture. The symmetrical, rectangular main room features a barrel-vaulted ceiling. A row of Corinthian columns on one side opens into a semicircular apse lined with bookshelves. Beautifully decorated in a color scheme of white, muted blue, and red with gold highlights, Adam's library is essentially an ancient Roman interior modified to meet the needs of an upper-class 18th-century gentleman.

It was probably inevitable that Lord Burlington, Robert Adam, and other leading English neoclassicists would exert an influence on builders in England's colonies. When the 13 American colonies broke away and became the United States in 1776, that influence remained strong. There, the neoclassical and Palladian styles became known as Georgian. Among the leading early U.S. architects was Thomas Jefferson, author

Monticello has been turned into a museum that the public can visit.

A HIGHLY REGARDED FIGURE

Born in Scotland, Robert Adam is often called the greatest architect of the late 18th century and the leading proponent of the neoclassical architectural style. His interest in designing buildings came from his father, an architect and stonemason. Adam's younger bother, James, also became an architect, and the two eventually became partners in a family architectural firm. After getting an education in Britain, Adam spent long periods in France and Italy studying ancient Roman ruins, which inspired him to use classical elements in contemporary buildings. Many of these elements, including Greco-Roman columns, pediments, and domes, came to grace the upper-class British homes Adam built or remodeled. His surviving drawings are now on display in Sir John Soane's Museum in London.

of the Declaration of Independence and the new country's third president. Construction of Jefferson's home, which he called Monticello, began in Virginia in the late 1700s. It was inspired by Chiswick House and other Palladian structures. Monticello's front porch features four Doric columns topped by a simple pediment; a modest but lovely dome resting on an octagonal red brick base rises from the center of the house.

Jefferson used a similar design, though on a larger scale, for the rotunda of the University of Virginia, completed in 1826. His love for the Greco-Roman style is evident in a statement he made about how he felt the yet-to-be-built U.S. Capitol should look: "Whenever it is proposed to prepare plans for the Capitol, I should prefer the adoption of some one of the [classical] models of antiquity which have had the [approval and praise] of thousands of years."[25]

GOTHIC REVIVAL

Although neoclassicism was a major force in architecture in the 18th and 19th centuries, it was not the only style chosen for monumental buildings. Many Gothic-style structures were also built in this period. Although less popular than the

Renaissance style in the 15th and 16th centuries, Gothic architecture did not completely die out in Europe, and a few Gothic buildings were built during the baroque period. For example, the universities of Cambridge and Oxford in England added several Gothic-style structures in the 1600s. Then in the 18th century came the emergence of Gothic literature, which romanticized the medieval era. This stimulated a reawakening of interest in Gothic architecture, a popular movement that came to be called the Gothic revival or the neo-Gothic style. Some scholars estimate that more Gothic-style buildings were constructed after 1750 in Europe and North America than were built in medieval times. These buildings could be either practical or fun. For instance, Cinderella Castle at Walt Disney World is an example of a Gothic revival building.

One of the most famous Gothic revival buildings is the British Parliament building in London, which was rebuilt in the Gothic revival style after a fire destroyed most of the old building in 1834. The 316-foot (96 m) clock tower on the northeast end of the building is often called Big Ben, but this is actually the name of the largest bell inside the clock tower. The tower itself is named Elizabeth Tower. However, many people still use Big Ben to refer to both the bell and the tower. Today, visitors come from all over the world to see Big Ben and the Houses of Parliament.

Some of the later structures of the Gothic revival possessed a crucial quality that no earlier versions did: They had partial or full iron frames. The Industrial Revolution, which flourished in Europe and North America in the 1800s, introduced new, stronger, more flexible building materials, including iron, which began to be used extensively in railways, bridges, and ships. This was the beginning of the technological and scientific innovations that led to modern-day architecture. The end of the Gothic revival created an interesting opening for new and very different architectural advances.

In the realm of monumental architecture, the Crystal Palace was particularly influential. Designed by Joseph Paxton and built in London's Hyde Park for the Great Exhibition of

This picture shows what the Crystal Palace looked like.

1851, it was 1,850 feet (560 m) long, 110 feet (33 m) high, and covered 25 acres (10 ha). The Crystal Palace was composed almost entirely of iron girders and large glass panels. This advanced and innovative mode of construction foreshadowed the widespread use of iron girders and glass in the modern era.

However, the Crystal Palace demonstrated more than the potential of iron and glass in building construction. It also showed the enormous usefulness of prefabricated materials, or premade, mass-produced units. Such units could be made in a factory by the hundreds or thousands, shipped to a construction site, and assembled according to the architect's preset plan. By using prefabricated units, the Crystal Palace took only nine months to build. Moreover, it could be easily dismantled and moved. In fact, it was moved to a new location a few years after the Great Exhibition closed. The building was destroyed by a fire in 1936.

The use of prefabricated materials in buildings made it possible for many more buildings to be made more quickly and cheaply than before. In the past, bricks, stones, glass windows, and other building materials had to be shaped by hand. Today, they can be made in a factory by machines. With this limitation removed, architects in the present can focus more on their designs and worry less about how long and difficult the construction process will be.

EMBRACING TRADITION

While architecture in some places has changed every few hundred years, in other places, people have mainly stuck with one style of architecture for hundreds or even thousands of years. When people find something that works, they often feel no need to change it. One example is the yurt, which has been used in parts of Central Asia for more than 2,000 years. It is particularly associated with Mongolia. Although the capital city of Ulaanbaatar has buildings just like those that can be found in any other city, many people in the country still make a living herding horses, yaks, or goats. This means their houses must be portable so they can move easily with their herds. A ger (the Mongolian word for yurt) is a round, tent-like structure that is big enough for an entire family to live in. The frame is made of wood and can be taken apart and put together quickly and easily. Felt that has been waterproofed is put over the frame to keep the heat in, and the door is often beautifully painted. Gers are kept warm with stoves that burn coal or wood.

Mongolian gers are often richly decorated inside and out.

CHAPTER SEVEN

THE 20TH AND 21ST CENTURIES

New inventions and scientific advancements made completely different styles of architecture possible starting in the late 19th century. These became commonplace in the 20th and 21st centuries. The most significant innovation was the use of iron and glass in construction. This opened up a whole new set of possibilities for both design and construction in modern architecture. Several other technological innovations were discovered during the Industrial Revolution that helped further the advances of architecture.

Another advancement was the elevator, which was invented in the 1850s and made widely available by 1880. This invention allowed construction workers as well as those who would later use a building to reach higher levels with ease. Two other advancements were new materials: steel and reinforced concrete. Steel was produced by adding small amounts of carbon to iron, which made it harder and more flexible. This, in turn, increased its strength. Reinforced concrete was made by adding iron or steel rods to concrete, greatly increasing its strength and stability. On the advantages of reinforced concrete, engineer and architect Mario Salvadori wrote,

> *It can be poured into forms and given any shape suitable to the channeling of loads. It can be sculpted to the wishes of the architect … It is economical, available almost everywhere, fire-resistant, and can be designed to be lightweight*

"Adaptive reuse" is a term that describes using an old building for a new purpose as people's needs change over time. One example is this McDonald's in a historic building in Paris, France.

> *to reduce the dead load or to have a whole gamut [range] of strengths to satisfy structural needs.*[26]

Prefabricated iron and concrete helped transform the possibilities of architectural construction, which led to the creation of a more diverse set of styles that are used around the world today. They were used to construct the Eiffel Tower in Paris. Designed by French architect Alexandre-Gustave Eiffel and completed in 1889, it is 1,063 feet (324 m) high, counting the antenna that was later added to turn it into a radio tower. The tower's 8,000-ton (7,200 mt) mass rests on four immense concrete foundations buried in the ground beneath the structure. The Eiffel Tower, which became an enduring French landmark, remained the tallest human-made structure in the world for the next 41 years.

In the late 1880s, some architects began to use these modern advances in big commercial and civic buildings to create large amounts of interior space. Importantly, the tensile strength of steel and reinforced concrete removed the need for the outer walls of these structures to bear a large portion of the overall load. Instead, most of the load could be distributed evenly through an interior framework made of steel and strengthened by reinforced concrete. In turn, this allowed architects to concentrate on added vertical height without fear of the structure collapsing. This started the trend of constructing taller buildings, which eventually led to the creation of the skyscraper.

TALLER THAN EVER

Since the early leading proponents of this new approach were architects based in Chicago, Illinois, it became known as the Chicago style, which flourished from the late 1880s to about 1930. A big factor in this approach stemmed from the gathering of several Chicago-based architects. This gathering became known as the First Chicago School. The group consisted at first of five men: Daniel Burnham, William LeBaron Jenney, John Root, Dankmar Adler, and Louis Sullivan. "Chicago school" is a term that references the specific style of architecture created by these men during this period of time and at this particular place. This group was seen as innovators, bouncing ideas back and forth, hoping to create a new, monumental style of architecture. In 1871, large portions of the city had been demolished in the Great Chicago Fire. This essentially created a clean slate for architects to build new structures. In turn, this opportunity created the beginning of skyscrapers being built around the city for the first time.

The world's first skyscraper was Chicago's Home Insurance Building, designed in the 1880s by William LeBaron Jenney. It had 10 stories and stood 138 feet (42 m) high. In 1890, 2 more stories were added, making it 180 feet (55 m) tall. Although 12 stories seems small compared to the skyscrapers that are typically built today, at the time it was unheard-of for a building to be that tall.

The building has been described in this way:

[Jenney's] revolutionary design utilized an inner skeleton of vertical columns and horizontal beams made out of steel. This was in stark contrast to earlier structures, which were supported by heavy masonry walls. Steel was not only lighter than brick, but it could carry more weight … As a result, the walls of the building didn't have to be as thick, and the structure could be much higher without collapsing under its own weight. Buildings with this type of frame could also have more windows, as the steel frame supported the building's weight and the stone or brick exterior merely acted as a "skin" to protect against weather.[27]

The Home Insurance Building not only set the model for construction of other buildings, but also determined what features those buildings would have, such as elevators and indoor plumbing.

These large commercial structures featured a fair amount of traditional architectural decoration on their exteriors. For example, the Masonic Temple, another Chicago building, had a front door that was encased in a Roman-style stone arch, with smaller decorative arches on either side. Meanwhile, the top few floors and roof were heavily decorated with modified Gothic and classical elements.

The early years of the 20th century witnessed not only increasingly tall steel-framed buildings, but also a continuation of the use of these sorts of traditional outer decorations. Appropriately, some architectural historians came to call such structures "traditionalist." Like much of the architecture created over the decades prior to this, it took solid ideas and concepts from past civilizations and adapted them to fit present-day styles and innovations.

A series of early skyscrapers in New York City followed the traditionalist style. The Woolworth Building, raised in 1913 and designed by Cass Gilbert, surpassed the Home Insurance Building in height. It stands 792 feet (241 m) high and cost $13.5 million to build, which at the time was a considerable amount of money. Gilbert purposely gave the structure a Gothic look by placing a Gothic-style tower on top of its lower half, which

The top of the Chrysler Building showcases the art deco style.

consists of a massive rectangular base. Though it is an office building, its resemblance to a Gothic cathedral has inspired some people to call it a "cathedral of commerce."

The Woolworth Building remained the tallest building in the world until 40 Wall Street and the Chrysler Building were built from 1928 to 1930. The Chrysler Building, at a height of 77 stories and 1,046 feet (319 m), was not only the tallest building in the world at the time but also the tallest structure, surpassing the Eiffel Tower. Designed by William Van Alen, the new skyscraper was a particularly successful traditionalist structure with some unique and quirky traits that put it in a class by itself. These traits were part of a then-popular artistic style called art deco. It was characterized by an eclectic combination of geometric shapes with an immense amount of ornamentation, all influenced by machines and machine parts. Art deco also featured liberal use of shiny aluminum, stainless steel, and interior spaces decorated with metallics.

Each material used in an art deco style was meant to portray a sense of wealth or power.

The Chrysler Building did not hold onto its title of world's tallest structure for long. In May 1931, New York's Empire State Building was completed. Another traditionalist skyscraper in the art deco style, it was designed by the architectural firm of Shreve, Lamb, and Harmon. It has 102 stories, stands 1,250 feet (381 m) tall—1,454 feet (443 m) including a broadcast tower later added at the top—and has 6,514 windows and 73 elevators.

AN INNOVATIVE AMERICAN

Less traditional in his approach to designing buildings was the American architect Frank Lloyd Wright, widely viewed as one of the leading and most influential architects of the 20th century. He was initially trained in the Chicago style and, for a while, worked with leading proponents of that approach, including Louis Sullivan. Soon, though, Wright struck out on his own. Thereafter, with some notable exceptions, he concentrated more on private houses and smaller structures rather than office buildings and other monumental structures. However, like the architects of larger buildings, Wright used modern materials, including steel frames, reinforced concrete, and glass panels. Wright's smaller structures also incorporated stone, wood, and other natural materials in an effort to appeal to the needs and comforts of the families who lived in them.

After attending an engineering school in Wisconsin in 1887, Wright moved to Chicago and joined a respected architectural firm. Six years later, he left the firm and set up his own practice in Oak Park, a Chicago suburb. By 1910, he had designed about 50 homes, mostly in the immediate region. Between 1910 and 1917, he designed many more houses in what came to be called the Prairie style.

The best known of the many private residences Wright designed were built between 1935 and 1939. However, his masterpiece remains the Solomon R. Guggenheim Museum in New York City, completed in 1959, shortly before his death.

Wright enjoyed using natural materials in the homes he designed, including Taliesin West, his own winter home (shown here).

Wright's houses typically featured extensive use of terraces covered by overhanging roof sections. An important example of his Prairie style architecture is the Robie House in Chicago, built in 1910. Made of fired bricks, sandstone slabs, wood, and glass, it is now a national historic landmark.

The most famous of Wright's private dwellings is Fallingwater, built for Mr. and Mrs. E.J. Kaufmann in Bear Run, Pennsylvania. The goal was to place the occupants as close to nature as possible. This was accomplished by setting the house in a thick stand of trees and allowing a stream with a waterfall to run directly beneath part of the house. Wright's attempt to make buildings seem to grow naturally out their surroundings became known informally as "organic" architecture. Modified versions of Wright's houses were copied by house

THE GUGGENHEIM

The Solomon R. Guggenheim Museum in New York City was one of several museums created to house the extensive art collection of the Guggenheim Foundation. In 1943, Frank Lloyd Wright was commissioned to design the structure. After years of design and construction, the museum opened on October 21, 1959. An elevator brings visitors to the top of the building, beginning their journey through the gallery from top to bottom. Wright shaped the space of the interior below with a rounded, ramp-like walkway that leads patrons back down to the first level. These rounded dimensions give a new outlook on the art that the building holds. Visitors are able to see the works not only head on, but from above and below as well. This building remains one of the best examples of interior and exterior architecture creating an incredible experience for each person that enters a building.

The structure of the Guggenheim gives visitors a unique experience.

builders across the United States and beyond all through the 20th century.

NEW AND DIFFERENT

Meanwhile, in the realm of larger-scale, commercial architecture, the Chicago and traditionalist styles were giving way to a new form known as modernism. Modernist architects wanted to stray away from the older styles in an attempt to create something new and different. The newer style had a more formal, structured look and often consisted of clean, simple looking designs. Extreme decoration of architectural elements was left behind and replaced with a very straightforward style that was still beautiful, just in different ways. Modernist buildings used a lot of steel, glass, concrete, and prefabricated, mass-produced materials. Modernist architects also promoted an idealistic notion that this new style would serve the needs of and please the vast majority of the general public, as opposed to previous structures that were created with the sole purpose of pleasing a god or nobility. In that regard, they expressed a style that promoted both function and beauty, creating exterior and interior spaces that pleased the masses and influenced architecture in the years to come.

Among the more important early proponents of modernism were France's Charles E. Jeanneret, nicknamed "Le Corbusier," and Germany's Walter Gropius and Ludwig Mies van der Rohe. They were strongly influenced by Frank Lloyd Wright.

The new movement began in the years following World War I and reached its stride between 1930 and 1960. During these years, it became the most dominant style in the world for large-scale civic and commercial structures, especially in Europe, North and South America, and the Soviet Union. For this reason, it came to be called the international style.

Thousands of large buildings were built in this architectural form. Among the more familiar commercial versions are the United Nations (UN) headquarters (1952), the Seagram Building (1958), Lever House (1952), and the Pan Am

Building (1963), all in New York City, as well as AMA Plaza (1973) in Chicago. The style was also widely used for giant urban housing projects in cities across the globe.

CONTROVERSIAL IDEAS

Despite the idealism and high hopes of modernist architects, the simplistic, supposedly futuristic international style did not last for centuries. In fact, it mostly went out of style by the early 1980s. This was partly because many of the people who worked and lived in these buildings found them neither functional nor comfortable. Indeed, critics called them plain, lacking in emotional feeling, and even dehumanizing.

As a result, the last two decades of the 20th century and first decade of the 21st century witnessed a new revolution in world architecture. Searching for a convenient label, some experts have called it postmodernism. Others prefer the term "second modernism." Still others emphasize that the movement contains diverse styles; as Neal put it, "Architecture went in many directions, with no single style dominant ... [so it] can be described best as Pluralism."[28]

Among the world's greatest architects, Frank O. Gehry is also one of the most controversial. Gehry became famous for his unconventional designs, many of which feature metal surfaces twisted into strange curves and bulging surfaces, often made of shining titanium or other metals. These designs would not have been possible to make in ancient times because they require computer programs to calculate the angles at which the walls need to bend. If the calculations were wrong, the whole building would collapse.

Many regard one of these structures, the Guggenheim Museum in Bilbao, Spain—not to be confused with the Solomon R. Guggenheim museum in New York City—as his masterpiece. This building became instantly famous and helped save the economy of Bilbao by attracting millions of tourists. However, Gehry has achieved nearly equal fame for his Dancing House in Prague, Czechia, the oddly twisted

Many of Frank Gehry's designs have sharp corners and boxy angles. This apartment building in Germany is made to look like imperfectly stacked blocks.

contours of which are meant to resemble two dancers. Many observers, fellow architects and other people alike, have strongly criticized Gehry's work, saying that it lacks harmony, is not organic enough, or is simply too weird for most people's tastes. However, others call him a visionary. This outlook represents much of architectural criticism today. Each person has different likes and opinions, so structures that take risks and stray away from the norm are regarded differently by the public.

Whatever one chooses to call it, the new trend in monumental architecture has so far been characterized by an effort to make buildings more accessible to people and their needs and comforts. In part, this has involved an emphasis on beauty to make people feel happy or admiring when they look at a building. For instance, architects reintroduced color in both interiors and exteriors, and they added various forms of decoration, including an old standby—

Greco-Roman columns. For example, in an addition to the Oberlin College Art Museum in Oberlin, Ohio, architect Robert Venturi filled an open space with an enormous, purely decorative, modified version of a Greek Ionic column. Such touches are more than just attractive. They also give people entering such buildings visual and emotional connections to the greatest cultural achievements of humanity's past. In addition, many of the newer buildings are designed in free-flowing, complex, highly asymmetrical shapes.

THINKING OF THE FUTURE

As the world has grown more aware of the dangers of climate change, there has been a demand for architecture that limits the amount of damage the structure will do to the planet. Things that people take for granted, such as lights, electricity,

SO YOU WANT TO BE AN ARCHITECT

Courtney Creenan-Chorley, AIA, the president of the Buffalo Architecture Foundation in New York, was inspired to become an architect by Frank Lloyd Wright. She said, "Growing up, I always loved drawing, building things, and exploring. In middle school, I went on a field trip to see homes Frank Lloyd Wright designed in Buffalo. Being in a space that was carefully designed was so inspiring that it made me want to learn more and design myself." She has this advice for people who are considering becoming architects:

> *Try new things, like different classes or after-school programs. You never know what will interest you. All classes contribute to studying architecture: math, science, art, history, English. Architecture has so many specialties that once you start practicing, the possibilities are endless ... it's great because you continue to learn new and different things constantly.*[1]

The AIA after Creenan-Chorley's name stands for American Institute of Architects. It shows that she is a registered architect and a member of the institute.

1. Courtney Creenan-Chorley, e-mail interview by author, January 30, 2017.

The Museum of Tomorrow in Brazil is designed to be open and airy, which reduces the need for air conditioning.

and plumbing, all have an impact on the planet, and most factories actively pollute the air. Buildings that use solar power to create energy, recycle wastewater instead of sending it back into the ground, and use plants to purify the air are in high demand. The challenge for architects today is to incorporate these features into their designs in a way that is still pleasing to the eye.

One architecture firm that is committed to sustainable, beautiful architecture is Bjarke Ingels Group (BIG), founded by Bjarke Ingels in 2005. BIG has designed several buildings around the world in ways that reduce their carbon footprint—the amount of carbon dioxide they release into the air as a result of using energy to power the lights, air conditioning, refrigerator, and other appliances. For instance, the company designed a resort to "look like manmade mountains with strips of green roof that keep the balconies 5 degrees Celsius cooler than they would be with conventional roofs."[29] Other companies have designed buildings to do things such as power themselves with solar panels and wind turbines, conserve water, and keep heat and air conditioning from escaping the building so less needs to be used. As technology evolves and people gain a better understanding of what is harming the planet and how to fix it, architecture will continue to change to meet those needs.

THE FUTURE OF ARCHITECTURE

The advances of architecture have come a long way since the first glimpses of civilization. Technological and scientific advancements have made it possible to create structures that were impossible to build a few centuries ago. As civilization has progressed, architectural needs have expanded—from a simple hut for shelter to large-capacity meeting halls and entertainment centers. Stylistic changes in each architectural movement advanced along with people's needs. Throughout the history of architecture, basic concepts such as the post and lintel have been adapted to present-day structures.

Today, architecture is seen as both a necessary means of providing shelter and an art form. Progression of this form throughout history has begun to create a balance between form and function, allowing each structure to provide an individual with much more than just a building. A structure can now reflect personal preferences or a community's needs and opinions. Today, architects have the opportunity to look back on historical structures and practices in order to adapt them into something modern. As societies change over time, architecture will always change along with them.

NOTES

INTRODUCTION: A BRIEF HISTORY

1. Vitruvius, *On Architecture*, trans. Frank Granger, vol. 1. Cambridge, MA: Harvard University Press, 2002, p. 7.
2. Vitruvius, *On Architecture*, vol. 1, p. 35.
3. Quoted in H.W. Janson and Anthony F. Janson, *History of Art: The Western Tradition*. New York, NY: Harry N. Abrams, 1997, p. 630.
4. James Neal, *Architecture: A Visual History*. New York, NY: Sterling, 2001, p. 6.
5. Courtney Creenan-Chorley, e-mail interview by author, January 30, 2017.
6. Neal, *Architecture*, p. 7.
7. Quoted in John Peter, *The Oral History of Modern Architecture: Interviews with the Greatest Architects of the Twentieth Century*. New York, NY: Harry N. Abrams, 1994, p. 128.

CHAPTER ONE: EARLY ARCHITECTURE

8. Marvin Trachtenberg and Isabelle Hyman, *Architecture: From Prehistory to Postmodernity*. New York, NY: Prentice-Hall, 2002, p. 47.
9. William R. Biers, *The Archaeology of Greece*. Ithaca, NY: Cornell University Press, 1996, p. 29.

CHAPTER TWO: REGIONAL STYLES

10. Neal, *Architecture*, p. 15.
11. Francis D.K. Ching et al., *A Global History of Architecture*. New York, NY: Wiley, 2006, p. 169.
12. Quoted in Charles Higham, *The Civilization of Angkor*. Berkeley, CA: University of California Press, 2004, pp. 1–2.
13. Quoted in Chris Scarre, ed., *The Seventy Wonders of the Ancient World*. London, UK: Thames and Hudson, 1999, p. 212.
14. Frederick Hartt, *Art: A History of Painting, Sculpture, and Architecture*. New York, NY: Prentice-Hall, 2003, p. 59.

CHAPTER THREE: THE GREEKS AND ROMANS

15. Neal, *Architecture*, p. 11.
16. Anita Abramovitz, *People and Spaces*. New York, NY: The Viking Press, 1979, p. 54.

CHAPTER FOUR: MEDIEVAL ARCHITECTURE

17. Sidney Toy, *Castles: Their Construction and History*. New York, NY: Dover, 1985, p. xiii.
18. Quoted in Janson and Janson, *History of Art*, p. 383.
19. Michael Raeburn, *Architecture of the World*. New York, NY: Galahad, 1975, p. 34.
20. Janson and Janson, *History of Art*, p. 322.
21. L. Sprague de Camp, *The Ancient Engineers*. New York, NY: Random House, 1995, p. 359.

CHAPTER FIVE: THE RENAISSANCE PERIOD

22. Neal, *Architecture*, p. 20.
23. Hartt, *Art*, p. 631.

CHAPTER SIX: LATER STYLES

24. Christine Paxman, *From Mud Huts to Skyscrapers: Architecture for Children*. New York, NY: Prestel, 2013, p. 26.
25. Quoted in Saul K. Padover, ed., *Thomas Jefferson and the National Capital*, letter dated April 10, 1791. Washington, DC: U.S. Government Printing Office, 1946, p. 59.

CHAPTER SEVEN: THE 20TH AND 21ST CENTURIES

26. Mario Salvadori, *Why Buildings Stand Up: The Strength of Architecture*. New York, NY: Norton, 1990, pp. 66–67.
27. History.com staff, "Home Insurance Building," History.com, 2010. www.history.com/topics/home-insurance-building.
28. Neal, *Architecture*, p. 32.
29. Megan Gambino, "Designing Buildings For Hot Climates, Cold Ones and Everything in Between," Smithsonian, February 5, 2015. www.smithsonianmag.com/innovation/designing-buildings-for-hot-climates-cold-ones-and-everything-in-between-180954003/.

FOR MORE INFORMATION

BOOKS

Allen, Peter. *Atlas of Amazing Architecture: The Most Incredible Buildings You've (Probably) Never Heard Of.* London, UK: Cicada Books Ltd., 2021.

This book introduces readers to hidden architectural gems.

Chaodong, Li. *Fantastic Chinese Architecture.* Montreal, Canada: Royal Collins Publishing Group Inc., 2023.

Learn more about Chinese architecture with the help of this book.

Velcovský, Tom. *From Pyramids to Palaces: Architecture Around the World.* Prague, Czech Republic: Albatros Media, 2024.

This book gives readers a tour of examples of building styles from across the globe.

Willkens, Danielle S. *Architecture for Teens: A Beginner's Book for Aspiring Architects.* Emeryville, CA: Rockridge Press, 2021.

Readers interested in a career as an architect can learn more about that path in this book.

WEBSITES

Ancient Greek Art

www.history.com/topics/ancient-history/ancient-greek-art

The History Channel provides an in-depth look into Greek art and architecture, which helped create the foundation of architectural history.

Ancient History Encyclopedia: Architecture Timeline

www.ancient.eu/timeline/architecture/

This detailed timeline lists important events in architectural history.

Arch Daily

www.archdaily.com

This website, created by and for architects, gives examples of recent architectural innovations.

Arch for Kids

www.archforkids.com

This website helps aspiring architects find programs to help them learn the skills they need to succeed in the field.

Britannica: Frank Lloyd Wright

www.britannica.com/biography/Frank-Lloyd-Wright

This resource offers a detailed account of Frank Lloyd Wright's life and architectural accomplishments.

INDEX

PICTURE CREDITS

Cover YURII MASLAK/Shutterstock.com; Cover, p. 1 Evan Lorne/Shutterstock.com; Cover, pp 1-112. MOMO STOCK/Shutterstock.com; Cover, pp. 1, 3, 4, 6, 14, 27, 38, 52, 64, 77, 87, 101, 103, 105, 111, 112 Lars Poyansky/Shutterstock.com; p. 5 saiko3p/Shutterstock.com; p. 7 AC Manley/Shutterstock.com; p. 9 posztos/Shutterstock.com; p. 10 telesniuk/Shutterstock.com; p. 13 WillAshley/Shutterstock.com; p. 16 iremsukaya/Shutterstock.com; p. 18 Poojaydv/Shutterstock.com; p. 21 AlexAnton/Shutterstock.com; p. 22 McCarthy's PhotoWorks/Shutterstock.com; p. 25 Dziewul/Shutterstock.com; p. 29 Dmitry Rukhlenko/Shutterstock.com; p. 31 Horizonman/Shutterstock.com; p. 33 CK-TravelPhotos/Shutterstock.com; p. 35 TheZAStudio/Shutterstock.com; p. 37 IR Stone/Shutterstock.com; p. 42 Tymonko Galyna/Shutterstock.com; p. 45 Preto Perola/Shutterstock.com; p. 47 Marques/Shutterstock.com; p. 49 Stefano Tammaro/Shutterstock.com; p. 51 Brandon Bourdages/Shutterstock.com; p. 54 Kirill Skorobogatko/Shutterstock.com; p. 57 Samia Jahan/Shutterstock.com; p. 58 Kirk Fisher/Shutterstock.com; p. 59 Poelmans_R/Shutterstock.com; p. 60 Ben Gingell/Shutterstock.com; p. 63 Sarath maroli/Shutterstock.com; p. 67 Vladitto/Shutterstock.com; p. 68 Aerial-motion/Shutterstock.com; p. 69 Vunav/Shutterstock.com; p. 71 Alex_Mastro/Shutterstock.com; p. 72 Collection Maykova/Shutterstock.com; p. 74 Christoph Schaarschmidt/Shutterstock.com; p. 75 Anna Morgan/Shutterstock.com; p. 76 muratart/Shutterstock.com; p. 79 Mister_Knight/Shutterstock.com; p. 80 pbk-pg/Shutterstock.com; p. 82 eurobanks/Shutterstock.com;p. 85 https://commons.wikimedia.org/wiki/File:Crystal_Palace_from_the_northeast_from_Dickinson%27s_Comprehensive_Pictures_of_the_Great_Exhibition_of_1851._1854.jpg; p. 86 Eleanor Scriven/Shutterstock.com; p. 88 Iryna Makukha/Shutterstock.com; p. 91 Flystock/Shutterstock.com; p. 93 Carrie A Hanrahan/Shutterstock.com; p. 94 Xackery Irving/Shutterstock.com; p. 97 BGStock72/Shutterstock.com; p. 99 Ramirez Gomez/Shutterstock.com.

ABOUT THE AUTHOR

JENNIFER LOMBARDO graduated from the University at Buffalo with a degree in English. She currently resides in Buffalo, New York, where she is both a writer and an editor.